The Jewish Condition

Challenges and Responses — 1938-2008

William B. Helmreich
Mark Rosenblum
David Schimel
editors

Transaction Publishers
New Brunswick (U.S.A.) and London (U.K.)

Library of Congress Catalog Number: 2008001822
ISBN: 978-1-4128-0802-6
Printed in the United States of America

Library of Congress Cataloging-in-Publication Data

The Jewish condition : challenges and responses--1938-2008 / [edited by] William B. Helmreich, Mark Rosenblum, and David Schimel.
        p. cm.
Includes bibliographical references and index.
ISBN 978-1-4128-0802-6 (alk. paper)
    1. Jews--Identity--History--20th century. 2. Jews--Identity--History--21st century. 3. Jews--Politics and government--20th century. 4. Jews--Politics and government--21st century. 5. Jews--United States--Politics and government--21st century. 6. Jews--United States--Politics and government--20th century. 7. Jews--Historiography. I. Helmreich, William B. II. Rosenblum, Mark. III. Schimel, David.
DS143.J4552 2008
305.892'4009045--dc22
                                                            2008001822

Contents

Introduction

William B. Helmreich

In April of 2007, a conference was held at Queens College regarding the state of world Jewry. None of us who organized the event had any idea as to the interest level among Jews for this topic. What we knew was that The Center for Jewish Studies had invited speakers each year to present lectures on Jewish subjects and that they had drawn an average audience of 150-200 participants

To our amazement, *more than 1,000 people* showed up. Several hundred who could not be accommodated in the main auditorium, watched the proceedings on video and an additional 250 people were, regrettably, turned away. This would have been a wonderful turnout anywhere but at Queens College it was remarkable. Unlike Manhattan's 92nd Street Y, there was no real history of such conferences and the college, with no subway line reaching it, was not that accessible.

To be sure, the array of speakers, among them Norman Podhoretz, Michael Walzer, Irving Louis Horowitz, Malcolm Hoenlein, and Alan Dershowitz, was impressive. But, as conversations with the attendees revealed, the main impetus for the turnout was a certain level of concern, even *angst*, not seen in the Jewish community in many years. With all that had been achieved by Jews, people wondered, did they have good reason to fear for their safety and security? And they wanted these distinguished leaders and scholars to answer that question.

What fueled these concerns is difficult to say. A major factor would have to be the bellicose statements made by Iran's President Ahmadinejad, threatening to wipe out Israel and his convening of an international conference challenging the fact that there had even been a Holocaust.

But there were other events too, of major significance, one of which was the 2006 conflict between Hezbollah and Israel. Israel has had numerous wars with its Arab neighbors, as everyone knows. What made this one different was the country's inability to defend its major population centers from attacks on its civilians. Hezbollah attacked Haifa, Israel's third largest city, and many other communities with impunity. The inconclusive end to the conflict, with many perceiving Israel as the loser, heightened Jews' sense of insecurity. Imagine if a sovereign nation like Syria or Egypt attacked the Jewish State, they wondered? Could it survive? Those who scoff at the basis for such doubts would be well advised to remember the dictum of the early sociologist, W.I. Thomas: "If men define situations as real, then they are real in terms of their consequences."

In Europe, Jews were become increasingly worried about the rising influence of Moslem communities hostile to Israel and Jews, and the seeming unwillingness of countries like France and England to confront them. Violence against Jews was reaching unprecedented heights and Jews, mostly in France, were beginning to leave in significant numbers.

These are broader events, and the essays in this volume speak to them. Originally presented at the conference, they have been revised for publication. They discuss and assess the threats facing both Jews and the Western world. While those writing are often in disagreement with each other, their differences tend to revolve around solutions to dilemmas, but almost never about their existence.

The conference theme raised the question of whether or not we are in a situation paralleling that of 1938, as Europe braced for the Nazi onslaught. None of the speakers thought so. Then again, neither did the conference conveners. Rather, the connection was suggested to provoke debate and it certainly did. Yet even as the speakers rejected the very idea of such a comparison, their presentations left many feeling that the Jewish community was facing some really serious issues and problems.

There were, in addition, other developments in the past year, that played an undetermined, but possibly pivotal role in raising the levels of anxiety in the Jewish community, and these could also account for the large turnout at this conference. Students of social movements will tell you that real concerns often find expression when accompanied by what the sociologist Neil Smelser called "precipitating events" that occur and there were plenty of them in the past year.

First there was the screed by Jimmy Carter. That a former President could rail against the Jews in an unbalanced book that was attacked for its shoddy research was deeply disturbing to many Jews. Even worse was the reluctance of some Jews to confront it. Brandeis University, an institution founded by Jews and academically committed to Jewish scholarship not only invited Carter to speak, but allowed him to dictate terms that violated the very principles of academic freedom he professed to champion. He spoke without challenge, without allowing anyone the opportunity to debate him.

Equally worrisome to many in the community was the widely publicized article (now a book) about the power of the Israel lobby, by John Mearsheimer of the University of Chicago and Stephen Walt of Harvard University. Few Jews would deny the existence of the lobby. What was upsetting was the charge that the lobby pressured the U.S. into support for Israel that was against its interests and that it exercised undue influence in pushing the U.S. into a war with Iraq.

Then there was the brutal murder in Paris by Moslems of Ilan Halimi, a young Jew who had been kidnapped. The horrific details of his torture and execution came to symbolize European anti-Semitism. Mel Gibson's tirade against Jews when arrested in Malibu for a traffic violation, also fanned fears and insecurities.

It is not possible to assess the impact of each of these events on every Jew, but the cumulative effect was probably there and played a role in making Jews feel that they needed to come together and reflect and debate the state of world Jewry today. Added to this was the ever-present fear of Jews that their future is endangered by assimilation.

The essays in this volume address these issues from a variety of perspectives. Some stake out ideological positions accompanied by justifications for them. Others present sobering and insightful analyses of the community and the problems it faces. What they all share in common is a level of seriousness that forces us to take notice. They are both optimistic and pessimistic, as well as realistic. But above all they are not despairing. Read carefully, they offer approaches and solutions that the community can both consider and adopt. That is why we have decided to publish them.

Preface

Mark Rosenblum

A few days prior to our conference, "Is it 1938 Again?" I received an inquiring phone call from a notable journalist and friend who was taken aback at what he perceived as the skewed nature of our program. Put off by the conference, he suggested that the title was a mantra from Bibi, and that the participants were predominantly his ideological fellow travelers, some of them "to the right of Attila the Hun." The inquiry was veering towards an inquisition when he decided to end ruefully with a question: "Mark, what am I missing here?"

He had not missed either former Prime Minister Netanyahu's rhetorical contribution to the conference, or the recognizable names from among the "who's who" of the conservative American Jewish intellectual community. However, he had missed pretty much everything else about the program: from the title, which ends with a question mark, not a period or an exclamation mark, to the ideological orientation of nearly half the speakers, who were clearly in his political camp.

The title is a provocative invitation to serious and contentious discussion between some of the best minds from the right, left, and center on an issue that is raw and not going away. Multiple sides were represented not because we are devotees of some kind of insipid relativism that insists every point has an equally valid counterpoint, but because there are fundamental issues about which we as a community are resolutely unresolved. Too often these issues are explored in forums for the like-minded who gather to cheerlead, recite their best arguments, and send their embedded ideologues out to engage in political battle. Our hope was that we might clarify our differences and perhaps even discover some unexpected agreement.

Our hopes were realized from the very first dialogue between Malcolm Hoenlein and Leonard Fein. Their presentations and their exchange revealed some stark differences. One was drawn more to the peril of the present moment and the other to its promise. Their policy prescriptions were more often than not in conflict. Both invoked the past and anticipated the future, but with different emphasis. However, neither saw Israel nor Jewry without allies (including in the Arab and Islamic world) or resources in their quest for security and continuity.

The title of the conference was inspired by Binyamin Netanyahu, but the text that you will read in this book refers to Yitzhak Rabin and scores of others whose presence is filtered through the strategic lens of our distinguished and diverse group of participants.

The overflow crowd heard a broad range of perspectives that ensured almost everyone in the audience heard ideas and representations of reality that they endorsed as well as those that they disdained. There was some gnashing of teeth, rolling of eyes, and a few catcalls that required a salient intervention from the podium. But mostly there was great enthusiasm and intellectual engagement. Two days of hard questions and tough answers had created a consensus: the discussion should continue with some urgency.

With several notable exceptions, the participants dismissed a back to the future exercise. The past is not prologue. The Jewish state of Israel exists and remains a formidable power. The United States, despite its beleaguered status, remains the world's sole superior power and a staunch ally of Israel. Most of the Sunni Arab regimes are more concerned about the challenges from the non-Arab state of Iran than from Israel. New fault lines may be emerging that create more policy options and greater security for Israel.

While it is not 1938, there is an annihilatory anti-Semitism that is on the prowl in 2007. The politicidal and genocidal language and policies of the government of Iran, and the charters and covenants of Hezbollah and Hamas are not aberrations. They are twenty-first-century existential threats. The question remains, what constitutes an effective strategy? Who are our allies, and how do we marshal our resources in order to effectively respond to the promise and peril of the new century?

Cognitive Dissonance or Denial?
Perhaps Both

David Schimel

NEW YORK (JTA) April 24, 2007 —With threats to the Jewish people emanating from so many directions—a nuclear Iran, the demographic challenges of American Jewry, the rise in anti-Semitic attacks around the world—a succession of leaders has warned that Jews face as much peril today as on the eve of the Holocaust. But when the Center for Jewish Studies at Queens College in New York City convened a conference this week on the state of world Jewry—ominously titled "Is it 1938 again?"—the consensus was a resounding "No."

An international array of Jewish scholars, writers, intellectuals and activists, including Norman Podhoretz and Michael Walzer, Alan Dershowitz and David Pryce-Jones, met before an overflow audience at Queens College on April 22 and 23 to assess, discuss and debate the State of World Jewry. As Conference Chair, I anticipated an exceptional opportunity for Jews representing a broad political spectrum to begin identifying areas of consensus and developing options for confronting dangers to Jewish survival.

What I had not anticipated was the rush to judgment by many in the Jewish media and several of the invited speakers. When facing the question, "Is It 1938 Again?" they responded with an emphatic, "No" and then proceeded to give responses that were complex, qualified and, at times, contradictory.

While the politically conservative speakers gave nuanced answers distinguishing between 1938 and today, they all agreed that contemporary World Jewry faces a global danger on a scale not seen since World War II.

Politically liberal presenters, on the other hand, were quick to assert that 2007 is not 1938, and then they went on to paradoxically acknowledge the worrisome developments that could potentially lead to a second Holocaust, particularly in the context of a nuclear-armed Iran, whose president threatens to "wipe Israel off the map." This acknowledgment was, in fact, the real consensus at the conference.

How then to explain the compulsion of some in the Jewish media and others who insisted that the conference's thematic question was answered with a resounding "No"? How do these "1938 Deniers," for lack of a better term, see the world?

One answer lies in the major differences expressed about the urgency or imminence of threats to World Jewry. Those (mainly political conservatives) who see today's conflict with global Jihadism as a threat as great as (or even greater than) that posed by Nazism believe that the West is already engaged in a world war and must act accordingly.

Most Jews of a politically liberal orientation believe that the threats are real but not imminent, compelling them to say it is not 1938 again. To believe otherwise leads to the inescapable conclusion that the situation faced by World Jewry requires dramatic and forceful action. It would also lead to a revision in thinking about the context of the current global struggle with Jihadism, including the Iraq war, something that most American Jewish leftists cannot bear to do.

Ironically, the response by "1938 Deniers" brings to mind the same willful denial that afflicted the forces of Western appeasement when Nazism confronted them throughout the 1930s (including 1938). It is easier to deny the immediacy of such danger than recognize it and take action. This mindset can be summed up as, "Whom are you going to believe, your political beliefs or your own lying eyes?"

"1938 Deniers" seem to be saying to themselves (and each other), 'yes the threat may be serious and real, but there is no need to get too perturbed.' As far as they are concerned the people who consider the situation ominous and urgent can be dismissed as alarmists. "1938 Deniers" consider the so-called "alarmists" to be, at best, over-reacting and, at worst, inappropriately belligerent, as if to say that the 'alarmists' rather than the Islamists represent an imminent danger. These political leftists are afraid that the "alarmists" will push them to take actions that they find allergic, especially if it involves use of military force. Hence they must attack the "neo-con" bogeymen who dare challenge their leftist worldview.

And a remarkable worldview it is. It tells us a great deal about the Weltanschauung of a wide segment, perhaps a large majority, of the American Jewish population some sixty years after the Holocaust. It is not reassuring.

For some time, it has been a quaint fact of American political life that Jews as a group consistently voted liberal Democratic, even when doing so was at variance with their own best self-interests, leading Milton Himmelfarb to famously quip, "Jews earn like Episcopalians but vote like Puerto Ricans."

In current circumstances, such pre-programmed thinking contributes to a collective failure to adequately respond to a growing and real threat to Jewish lives—first and foremost the six million Israeli Jews. Sixty years after the Holocaust, half of American Jews are disconnected from the Jewish community and its concerns. They blend themselves into an embracing American cultural and social fabric and are joined daily by a growing stream of many (mainly secular) Jews. A case, as it were, of safety in anonymity. The result is a far more tenuous link between American Jews and Israel.

In an act of cognitive dissonance, even many who do retain strong Jewish identities seem unwilling to see existential danger to Jews and the Jewish State even when it stares them in the face. The very idea of a repeat of the Holocaust seems too painful to confront; therefore the need to engage in self-deception.

What separates these two schools of thought, i.e., the "1938 Deniers" and those who they disdain as "neo-cons,'" comes down to the following: Neo-Cons believe in being safe rather than sorry, while "1938 Deniers" fear being sorry for forceful actions that may fall short of the ideal.

This then is the main conclusion of the "Is it 1938 Again?" conference: A major part of American Jewry today, just as in the 1930s, is in denial. As Martin Gilbert has noted about the war with radical Islam today, history does repeat itself.

1

Back to the Future: Is it 1938 Again?

Malcolm Hoenlein

The question that was posed was: is this 1938? I can give three answers: yes, no, and could be. It reminds me of when I came back the last time from Israel, and people said to me: "Tell me in a word how it was." I said "Good." They said, "Okay, okay, in two words." I said: "Not good."

So I'm not going to be able to summarize it quite that quickly, but I will try and address the three options. The real question I have is: do we really want to know? Recall that line from the movie *A Few Good Men*: "You want the truth? You can't *handle* the truth." I'm not sure that we're prepared to handle the truth. The truth is that the issue is not whether this is 1938 or 1936 or 1934 or 1932, as different people have claimed. What's important is what lessons we learned from that period that we apply today. No analogy is going to be perfect, maybe not even approximate. But what is relevant are the lessons we learned. That's why Judaism places such an emphasis on remembrance. Tomorrow is *Yom HaZikaron*, Remembrance Day. Last week we marked *Yom HaShoah*, Holocaust Memorial Day, and the word that was chosen to symbolize the Holocaust was not along the lines of "revenge" or "avenge"; it was "*Zachor*," remember There is no Hebrew word for history. It's *zechirah*, remembrance. And unique to Judaism is that remembrance applies to the future.

Winston Churchill once said, "The further back you look, the further ahead you will see." President Truman, I recently learned, said that the present is only the history you have yet to experience. *Chazal*, our sages, said it a thousand years earlier; they understood that experience was the best teacher and only those who look back could be equipped to look forward; that only those who learned the lessons of the past were prepared to meet the challenges of today and the opportunities of tomorrow.

1

For us, looking back is not about dwelling on the *tsuris*, the hardships, of the past. We remember them, but for us remembrance is about the future because we know that what we do today determines that future. Learning the lessons of the past enables us to spare future generations those trials and tribulations. If you go back to the Bible, you see that we're told of our forefathers and foremothers not just their great successes, but their frailties, too, because we are to learn from their experiences. Our whole calendar is geared to being experiential, not just to ritual observance. But we experience what previous generations went through in order for us to learn their lessons and their relevance to today. *Zechirah*, remembrance, calls on us to go back and look at the period of the 1930s, to understand what happened then. What went wrong? What were the failures? And how do we prevent ourselves from falling into the same traps again?

I believe that this is a watershed period in Jewish history—in world history, American history, too, but definitely in Jewish history. And so this volume is especially important for remembrance, specifically for trying to ascertain the truth that some of us don't want to wrestle with. So let me start by saying why this is not 1938. Obviously, first and foremost, because we have the Jewish State, with a strong army, with embassies around the world, with an ability to rescue Jewish communities. As we have seen in our lifetimes, the existence of the State of Israel makes possible the rescue of Russian Jews and Ethiopian Jews and Yemenite Jews and Syrian Jews and Iraqi Jews and Iranian Jews, many of whom were written off to Jewish history. So the fact that we have a Jewish state makes all the difference in the world. We have seen the ingathering of the exiles as a result of it, including the last victims of the Holocaust. We have seen that when Jews are in danger, Jewish communities are able to act because there is a Jewish state.

The anti-Semitism that we will talk about is not state-sponsored in most countries. And officials to significant degrees, at least in public pronouncements, renounce anti-Semitism. Anti-Semitism is not universal in all Muslim countries or communities. Furthermore, American Jews are not the same as in 1938. We are not Jews of silence. We are not driven by the same fears or concerns or restraints that at times characterized the Jewish leadership during the thirties and forties. We now have lobbies. We have Jewish activism. We showed it in the Soviet Jewry Movement and in so many other instances. Abba Eban wrote that in World War II Jews had influence in many places but power in none. Today Jews have power. The whole world describes that power today. In politics, it's not reality that counts, it's perception. And if the world says you are powerful, you are powerful, and that enables us to affect—even if we can't determine—the outcome. We also have a different U.S. government. Republicans and Democrats alike overwhelmingly, by a figure of more than 90 percent, stand up for Israel on virtually every bill. We have a president who, like previous presidents, is a great friend of Israel and of the Jewish people and we see that the American people reject anti-Semitism and that more than 70 percent of them, a record number since the creation of the state, express support for Israel. And lastly, there are tens of millions of Christians who stand with Israel and kneel.

So the question is: if all of this is so good, where does the "yes" come in? When we read the Haggadah on Passover, we recited the paragraph *"ve-hee she'amdah,"* which describes the enemies that arise in every generation. It does not use the past tense. It uses the present tense, describing the enemies "that *arise*...that seek to *destroy* us." This usage is to remind us that the enemies arise in every generation. They may have different geography or different language, different colors on their uniforms, but the enemies are the same. Rabbi Yaakov Kaminetsky asked a question: is it really true that in every generation there are enemies that arise to seek to destroy us? And his answer is taken from the next paragraph that follows in the Haggadah, *"tze u'lemad,"* go out and learn. It deals with the Biblical figure Lavan, who wanted to destroy everything because he wanted to root out a progenitor, Yaakov, the father of the tribes of Israel. Yaakov, Jacob, lived in relative wealth and prosperity, but he had to be reminded that even at that time, with the appearance of calm, there was an enemy planning and plotting against him. Even in periods when we have relative affluence and relative calm, we have to be reminded all the time of the potential dangers.

That is what *zechirah* is about—a constant reminder setting off the alarm, teaching us to look beyond the surface to see the underlying reality, which brings me to 1938. As I said there are no analogies that are perfect but there are similarities. There is an implacable enemy driven by an extremist ideology that seeks to wipe out the Jewish State and the Jewish people along with many others. It has the backing of a national government that is engaged in a global war, rallying and exploiting millions of people. When we look at the state of Iran, with its huge capacity in terms of weapons, power, missile capacity, ships, and planes, let alone its nuclear aspirations, when we see other great powers in the Arab world and in the Muslim world teetering, always in danger of falling into the hands of similar extremist regimes, when we see the Jihadi grand designs of Ahmadinejad and others, it gives rise to concern.

Many scholars, including Bernard Lewis, Robert Wistrich, and others, have shown that the Islamist ideology is very similar to Nazi ideology. I won't go into it now, but their books lay out both visions and show the similarities between them. We are still living in a world where apathy and indifference abound. Just look at the situation in Darfur. We live in a world where the big lie against Jews and Israel still works. We saw it during the war in Lebanon, with one distortion after another: from the 950 pictures that had to be taken out of the Reuters archives to the false story about the bombing of the ambulances by Israel, to the distortion about numbers and who was responsible, and so on. The difference from seventy years ago is that the big lie can be spread a lot faster. The fact that *The Protocols of the Elders of Zion* is the No. 2 best seller in the world after the Bible should be a warning. The difference is that the Nazis tried to hide their crimes. The Islamists advertise it. We see a transnational Jihadi Islam, not the Islam of the entire Muslim world, and we have to make the distinction. But truly that Islamism represents a danger to the Jewish people.

In addition, there is a media distortion that misrepresents Israel and the Jewish people all too frequently. We also see the intellectual justifiers of the Islamists, and corruption in general, in significant elements of the academy. We see those who continue to pursue the policy of appeasement, revealing that Europe, in particular, has learned little in the past seventy years. Indeed, recent statistics show that European trade with Iran has gone up 23 percent in the last two years. You've all seen the three years of negotiations—I should say humiliations—that they engaged in with Iran. You still see the scapegoating and the resurgence of anti-Semitism, the failure of governments to act effectively to root it out. There is a 60 percent increase in anti-Semitism this year in Austria, Germany, and other countries, including Canada and Australia. We see the failure to prosecute anti-Semitic crimes—less than one percent of those who commit acts of crime against Jews in Europe actually are prosecuted and convicted. We see the Jews in Israel being held not to a higher standard but to a double standard.

Now I want to get to the "could be." The "could be" relates to the potential of this period turning into something much more serious. As I said, I do not believe this is 1938. The differences that I described really do cast this period in a very different light. Bernard Lewis said that he is more worried today than he was in 1941 in England, and he is over ninety-one years old. To take the British example to heart, when we see the combination of traditional anti-Semitism, Islamic anti-Semitism, anti-

Zionism and anti-globalization, and of course anti-Americanism, coming together in this cocktail of hatred, the consequences are obvious—not only in the statistics that I cited but in many other ways, as well.

In particular, I for one question whether there is a future for Jews in Europe. The demographic statistics speak for themselves. Forty percent of the European births in this generation will be Muslim children. Look at the crime situation. In France alone, there were 50,000 acts of urban violence last year by Muslims; 1,000 cars a week torched; fifty police-men a week beaten up; some 1,400 ghettoes where Jews and Christians cannot live, and all of these are government statistics, not mine. This breakdown of law and order threatens Jews. When a European police chief was asked why he did not respond to the fire-bombing of a synagogue during riots last year, he replied, "Why would I? It happens every day." It took the government of France three weeks to acknowledge that Ilan Halimi had been a victim of an anti-Semitic crime in his brutal murder. True, the government has taken steps now, belatedly, for education and similar efforts. But to many, it's too late, and young French Jews are voting with their feet.

In Great Britain, this year, they broke all the records since they began keeping track of anti-Semitic attacks after World War II. The propor-tion of pro-Israel British is between 17 and 19 percent. It is no wonder that in Europe a recent poll showed that when asked which country is the greatest danger to world peace, Israel ranked No. 1, with over 50 percent of the respondents ranking the Jewish state ahead of Iran and many others. (The United States came in fourth, so they have to try harder.) When asked to describe the most disgusting country in the world, they similarly responded in a separate poll that it was Israel. And there is great fear of what will happen if there is a serious economic downturn in Europe. I was in Berlin a few weeks ago to attend a con-ference and several of the speakers spoke openly about their concern. The chief rabbi of Great Britain, not a man given to exaggeration, told of a *tsunami* of anti-Semitism in his country. And the proof of that is in the recent action this past week by the United Kingdom's National Union of Journalists. Although it only involved 120 or so of the 40,000 members, they voted to boycott Israeli products in the same week that their colleague Alan Johnston was being held in Gaza. And the BBC's Alan Hart, sixty-five years old with a distinguished career, said in his personal blog that the only one who had to gain from Johnston's dis-appearance was the Mossad, who perhaps concealed their operation in kidnapping Johnston.

Last year England's Academic Union voted to boycott Israel, and Irish cultural and academic associations have done similar things. We see the mayor of London engaging in anti-Semitic vitriol and then getting re-elected. Eighty-five percent of the reports on BBC were negative towards Israel and 15 percent were neutral, leaving not much room for positive support. It is what I call the poisoning of the elite. And it is imperative for us to understand it because I believe that what happened in Great Britain is happening here. And the reason you don't see it is because it's a cancer that spreads among the intellectual elite and then trickles down. Britain didn't start off with only 20 percent supporting Israel. That's an outgrowth of these campaigns.

Chief rabbis of France, Germany, and Norway have warned Jews not to go out wearing obvious Jewish symbols. And we have seen the statistics in Germany. A recent study found that 80 percent of Germans no longer feel that there is a special relationship with Israel and 44 percent expressed anti-Semitic views. In France, when they added a new channel to try and balance the reportage in French and in Arabic and a few other languages, they never mentioned Halimi. They never talked about the attacks on Jews. They never talked about anti-Semitism. And yet, one of the major producers wrote an article last week saying that so much anti-Semitic reaction was received that they shut down their response line. Indeed, we see the radicalization of the Muslim population. The failure of the European governments to properly integrate these populations has meant that their young people have become radicalized, even those of moderate and secular communities like the Turkish expatriates in Germany.

We have many other statistics but time does not allow me to cite them. We see the constant diet of incitement and its impacts. We see the kind of intimidation that results from it, such that you cannot get pro-Israel speakers on most British campuses, nor on most European campuses, and we know that people of that mindset don't speak out today in the ways that they should. The situation in Iran contributes to this development, not only because of its direct export of violence; indeed, they were responsible for the riots that took place in Great Britain. Consider what a foreign minister of one of Europe's largest countries said to me recently when I challenged him about why Europe is not standing up. He said, "What do you want from us? We have 20 million Muslims in Europe and you saw the riots." I asked him, "So you're telling us that intimidation works and the cancer will grow?"

Intimidation indeed works. The European response to it has been the same policy, the same kind of appeasement that drove Chamberlain to Munich, and Winston Churchill to tell him, upon his return, that in a choice between war and disgrace he chose disgrace. And, Churchill added, now you'll have war. Europeans have learned little. You see it in the attempts toward moderation and to avoid imposing the economic sanctions that the U.S. has worked out—which indeed are having an effect and which can bring about change. Not a military action, which would only be the result of a failure to take the kind of preventative steps, the kind of effective steps that the sanctions represent.

Hitler used academics and others too. Through them he tried to put responsibility for all the ills that grew out of World War I on the Jews, including the economic, social and political problems. He cut the Jews off from commerce, from education and from social intercourse with the world. These steps paved the way, shortly thereafter, for *Kristallnacht*, the night when we now know that 1,407 synagogues were destroyed. That, in turn, paved the way ultimately for the final solution. When 300 reporters gathered in the White House a week after *Kristallnacht*, and asked President Roosevelt what his reaction was, the president said: "I'm outraged." They asked him what he is going to do for German refugees, and he refused to answer, even as his cousin was then the secretary of immigration. His wife got up in front of Congress and, responding to a bill aimed at saving 20,000 German Jewish children, she remarked that 20,000 adorable children become 20,000 ugly adults. The bill was defeated. Hitler was reported to have told the Chief of Staff: "We're free to do what we want with the Jews. The world doesn't care."

Once again we see the same kind of accusations about Jewish control, about Jewish manipulation, promulgated in academia and in the elite —not only in Europe, but also here. It's easy to find blame. It's easy to scapegoat. It's much easier than trying to have to think through issues. There are social constraints today that didn't exist in the 1930's, so it is not appropriate yet to speak against Jews. But can one speak about the corporate entities that represent the Jewish people? Or can one claim "we're not anti-Semitic, we're only anti-Zionists"?

A recent study in Great Britain showed conclusively that anti-Zionism is really just a cover for anti-Semitism. That doesn't mean that you cannot be critical of Israel without being an anti-Semite. If that were the case, 99 percent of Israelis would be anti-Semites. You can be critical without being bigoted. But you cannot demonize, you cannot de-legitimize the state. You can hold it to a higher standard, as we all do, but not to an impossible standard. We have to think, therefore, about the nature and consequences of our criticism. We have to consider the intensity and the veracity and most of all how it is perceived, no matter what the source, even when that source comes from within the Jewish community. It has got to be thought through carefully.

The situation in the United States has deteriorated, I believe, and the trickle from the poisoning of the elite is first becoming visible. It is not always obvious, but what was marginally acceptable on the fringes a year ago is increasingly acceptable in the mainstream today. A lot of this grows out of the Durbin Conference. In 1999, the United Nations convened the conference to deal with Xenophobia, anti-Semitism and hatred. It turned into an orgy of anti-Semitism, anti-Israelism, and anti-Americanism. But what we saw there was the blueprint laid out. Just as they got rid of the South African apartheid state in the twentieth century, they predicted, they will get rid of the Zionist apartheid state in the twenty-first century. And everything we saw there, from divestment to the campaign to squelch and silence supporters of Israel, is increasingly in evidence here today.

They have created an interesting dilemma for us. If we don't speak out in response, they say, "You see? Everybody agrees." If we do speak out, they say "You see that? The Jewish Lobby and the Jewish community are squelching any kind of criticism." Indeed, in the past year we saw the publication of Stephen Walt and John Mearsheimer's original paper attacking the pro-Israel lobby. It did not appear in an American publication, though it was submitted to many; yet this was not because Jewish organizations objected—we didn't even know about it —but because none of the editors who read it felt it was worthy of publication. Ultimately they had to go to the *London Review of Books*, which sounds a lot more effective and important than it is. Still, less than a year later they received the largest advance ever given to a professor at Harvard, $750,000, for a book released in September, 2007. They're invited to campuses across the country and they are now joined by former president Jimmy Carter and his campus crusade. Carter recently told an audience that "as long as American politicians are seen as knee-jerk supporters of Israel, the country's role as the Middle East peace broker will be endangered." And he appealed to the audience to demand of their political representatives, to "pledge to you that they will take a balanced position between Israel and the Palestinians." And I need not tell you how many hundreds of thousands of copies his book sold and how many mistakes, historical mistakes, it contains. Others accuse him of plagiarism, and of many other things, but there is no one who claims that his book is historically accurate. Scott Ritter, meanwhile, is publishing a new book of his own, that will accuse us of being responsible for a war in Iran—and none has even taken place yet. Wesley Clark has stated that the war in Iraq was driven by so-called "New York money people."

In Great Britain, a Jew is four times more likely to be the victim of a hate crime than a Muslim. In the U.S., a Jew is seven times more likely to be the victim of a hate crime than a Muslim. And how much do you read about Islamophobia (which concerns us, as we should be concerned about attacks on any group), but how little is said about the attacks against Jews? In fact the war on terrorism is intricately linked to all this; many of the 500 terrorist operations in the U.S. have ties to anti-Semitic activities. And ads are being placed in places like the metro system in Washington D.C. to mark the fortieth anniversary of Israel's "occupation." We see many other campaigns on campuses across the country, including the "Israel Apartheid Week," which has led in some cases to violence against participants who dared to ask of the organizers whether they support terrorism. The Foreign Policy Association held a conference titled "A World Without Israel," and a study by that organization found that 68 percent of the foreign policy elite say the Jews have too much influence or too much power.

At so many campuses we find similar sentiment uttered by faculty members; in place of legitimate debate or criticism they choose one-sided diatribe. I was approached by faculty members at an Ivy League college who told me that they're being driven out for tenure by other faculty because they are too pro-Israel. This is an attempt to silence us, to blame the Jewish Lobby for every ill. It's a manipulation. It's a distortion. It's a misrepresentation. Indeed it is already causing damage. We will see, in fact, that it will come to a head with the AIPAC trial, which has no justification whatsoever: two people did nothing different from what thousands of people do in Washington every week and yet they have been investigated for more than seven years, their phones tapped, their lives interfered with, ultimately culminating in their arrest. Dorothy Rabinowitz in the *Wall Street Journal* described this case very aptly, in the headline reminding us: "First they came for the Jews..."

We see the "if only Israel" crowd promoting the view that if only Israel wouldn't defend its citizens, if only Israel would make more concessions, if somehow Israel didn't exist, all of the world's problems would go away. The Sunni-Shi'a battle of 900 years would go away. All of the other problems in the Arab world—everything—would disappear if only Israel did. We see the blame laid on "neo-cons," read "Jews," for the last war and for the (projected) next war, and part of the problem is that we have lowered the bar on tolerance of anti-Semitism. We tolerate it whether it's in textbooks or on campuses and other places.

The U.S. Commission on Civil Rights Public Education Campaign to End Campus Anti-Semitism reported just recently on the substantial anti-Jewish sentiment it discovered and of the need to take action. Similar results were found by the Interparliamentary Committee in Great Britain. The U.N. Human Rights Council issued eight edicts, all of them about one country violating human rights—not China, not Syria, not Iran—all of them about Israel. Again, it is one thing to criticize Israel; quite another to demonize it or de-legitimize it.

I think for the Jewish community this is a time when we are being tested. The child of forgetting, Menasheh, was blessed, while the child of remembrance, Ephraim, was blessed even more. Judaism places upon us the responsibility of history. Benjamin Disraeli once said that there's no faith more ghastly than that of a stupid Jew. He didn't mean our IQ's. He meant Jews who don't get it. Jews who don't see the world as it is, rather than as they would like it to be. Recall Hansen's Law, namely that the third generation seeks to remember what the second generation sought to forget.

This generation has to remember. It has to look back. We have to become more proactive. We have to make sure that anti-Semitism is confronted in whatever form it takes; not to tolerate it, not to excuse it. We have to hold government and law enforcement accountable. We have to engage in much greater educational efforts. We have to reach out, rebuild a coalition, and not take for granted the great numbers that we have now on our side. Jewish leaders and Jewish thinkers and community activists must act. Moses, when he gave us the *mitzvah* [commandment] of *Zachor*, advised us that the greatest danger to the Jews is not natural disasters or war; it's complacency and indifference that comes out of affluence. We blind ourselves to the reality. So the answer rests in what we do. Not even what *they* do, but what *we* do.

Recall the difference between Mount Sinai and the Temple Mount. With Mount Sinai we got the Torah. Immediately afterwards, Jews could go up and touch it. Yet with the Holy Temple Mount, to this day there are parts so holy that we are not supposed to go there. And the difference was that on Mount Sinai the Jews did not do anything. When they got the Torah, they said, *"Na'aseh ve'Nishmah,"* we accept it. But Abraham physically brought Isaac to the Temple Mount and was prepared to make the ultimate sacrifice there. The Jews by their sweat and tears and blood built two of the holy temples there. It's what man does to infuse the moment with sanctity that gives it its ultimate importance. Rabbi Soloveitchik said that God sanctified time, man sanctified space. Now we're in a time when we have to sanctify this space in history because future generations will judge us, just as we judge a generation of seventy years ago, and ask, What did they do? Your grandchildren will ask: What did you do? We are being tested in that regard. We have to maintain zero tolerance of anti-Semitism under any of its guises, and remembrance about the past and about the future. It is our future that's at stake.

2

Lessons from the Past: Hopes for the Future

Leonard Fein

Among the most popular songs of Judaism's new age in America is one whose words are attributed to Rabbi Nachman of Bratslav. "The whole world," he wrote, "is a narrow bridge, and the main thing is not to be afraid at all."

The melody is beguiling and the words are enticing. But the message is preposterous, especially these days. Not to be afraid at all? But these days there is a widespread and still growing sense that we are confronted by a rise in anti-Semitism, virtually worldwide. There's the ongoing scandal of the United Nations Human Rights Council; there's the vexing issue of Muslim anti-Semitism in France; there's Israel's low estate, as confirmed in the recent international survey that identifies Israel as the most dangerous nation on earth, more dangerous than North Korea, than the United States, than Iran. And there is, of course, Iran, the Iran that prompted Bibi Netanyahu to offer us a mantra that has been taken up as near-gospel by a wide swath of American Jewry.

In Netanyahu's words, "It's 1938, and Iran is Germany, and it's racing to arm itself with nuclear weapons. Same tendencies: to slander and vilify its victim in preparation for slaughter. Ahmadinijad takes his cue from Hitler, and no one cares. Every week he talks about erasing Israel from the map, and no one says anything."

Whether or not one accepts Netanyahu's inflamed rhetoric, the vilification aimed at Israel is real, the threats directed at Israel are serious, and the consequent distress, bordering on panic, we now experience is pervasive.

But in trying to sort all this out and to respond appropriately we come immediately upon a problem. While it is true that history can be a useful guide, it is not less true that history can be a trap. Santayana was right: "Those who forget history are condemned to repeat it." But the opposite of forgetting is remembering, not obsessing. Those who are obsessed by history are *as* likely to repeat it as those who forget it. And in dealing with Jewish fears, it is exceedingly difficult to know when we are using our history and when we have become history's prisoners.

I have in mind words many of us recited just a few weeks ago: "*She'lo echad bilvad amad aleinu l'chaloteinu, ela she'b'chol dor va'dor omdim aleinu l'chaloteinu*"—"it was not merely once that the others stood against us and sought to destroy us, but in every generation, there are those who stand against us and seek to destroy us."

The words are familiar, the sentiment they express an authentic part of our inherited tradition. So Nelly Sachs, Nobel Laureate in literature, 1966, could write, "We rehearse tomorrow's death even today while the old dying still wilts within us." So Philip Roth, in *The Anatomy Lesson*, could tell us of how the narrator's stricken mother was asked by her neurologist to write her name on a piece of paper. "She took the pen from his hand and instead of 'Selma' wrote the word 'holocaust,' perfectly spelled. This was in Miami Beach in 1970, inscribed by a woman whose writing otherwise consisted of recipes on index cards, several thousand thank you notes, and a voluminous file of knitting instructions…. But she had a tumor in her head the size of a lemon, and it seemed to have forced out everything except the one word. That it couldn't dislodge. It must have been there all the time without their even knowing it."

How can we distinguish between a tumor on the inside and a threat from the outside? Have we not been taught that to be a Jew is to live cramped between pogrom and pogrom, that ours is a partnership in persecution, an endless voyage of the damned, its sails filled with the winds of others' hatred? Are not threat and tumor alike familiar affirmations of Jewish identity? In short, is 1938 a caution or a snare?

As caution, the invocation of 1938 is entirely reasonable. Whatever the differences among the experts on whether Iran is seeking nuclear weapons and on when it may actually have the capability to manufacture them—and there are many differences—neither we nor the Israelis can run the risk of turning a deaf ear to the ominous assessments. The odds may be low, but the risks are too high to be thought acceptable.

That said, the mantrification of 1938 is hardly a policy or even an adequate foundation for a policy. It doesn't tell us whether to make ready for war or to seek more intensive and extensive negotiation. It implies sticks but is silent on carrots. It substitutes slogan for analysis. It is a radically incomplete, hence inadequate and even misleading, guide. Insofar as it ignores much of more recent history, it becomes not a caution, but a snare.

More recent history: is it not peculiar that the principal purveyor of the idea that this is 1938 is the former and perhaps even future prime minister of the sovereign state of Israel, the nation state that was founded precisely to excise the tumor, to break the tediously bloody cycle of our people's past, to be the place that signified our return to agency? The Jews of Israel, whatever their faults, individual and collective, are not the dead timber of a petrified forest impotently awaiting the gathering firestorm. And they are surely not the innocents of an earlier time, before that which could not have been imagined was imagined, before the Shoah, the Holocaust, was engraved on our consciousness, and the world's. Agency: they may not govern history; no one does. But they are able to bend it, if so they will.

As are we, here. We are hardly the timid Jews of 1938, or even of 1967. Towards the end of May of 1967, as we were seized by the fear of "another Auschwitz," the executive committee of Boston's Jewish federation gathered to consider whether to hold a mass rally of support for the apparently beleaguered Jewish state. The specific proposal was to hold such a rally on the Boston Common, in the heart of downtown Boston, where George Washington once camped. There being no precedent for such a public display, the debate was intense. Finally, a compromise was reached: the rally would go forward, but only on condition that it not be publicized. And that curious decision was followed by a still more intense debate regarding the propriety of singing *Hatikvah* at that rally.

Can anyone seriously imagine such timorous behavior in 2007? By now, we have chained ourselves to the gates of the White House on behalf of Soviet Jewry, on behalf of an end to apartheid, on Israel's behalf. We know our way to the housetops and how to shout when we reach them. And we know our way, as well, to and in the corridors of this nation's power.

Nor, for that matter, is our America the America of 1938. We are now a nation practiced in intervention, for better and for worse, and the thought of this nation abandoning Israel to a fiery fate is both base and baseless.

For all these reasons, it is time—and then some—to declare that the exile is over, that the one-lane and one-way path the "*golus*" Jew allegedly traveled is no longer our destiny, that we are free men and women, a free people, able to choose the direction for our journey. "Blind fool," they will say, "can't you see the existential threat? It's not just the nuclear weapons that may soon be in the hands of our malicious enemies, it is that everywhere we turn, Israel's very legitimacy is challenged, that the world cannot, even after all these years, accept the idea of a Jewish state. You and your utopian Labor Zionism, your reckless messianism, your fixation on the distant end of days. You want to know tomorrow's texture? Look to yesterday; that remains the most reliable guide we have."

But which is the yesterday we should choose to guide us? Is it September 29, 1938, the day the Munich agreement was signed, or is it September 13, 1993, on the south lawn of the White House where the Oslo accords were signed, or is it November 6, 1995, the day Yitzhak Rabin was buried?

Mark well Rabin's words on accepting the Nobel Prize for peace ten months before his assassination:

> We are witnessing a new wind blowing throughout the world regarding its relationship with the state of Israel: the claim that the "whole world is against us" has dissipated in the spirit of peace. The world is not against us. The world is with us.

And the best evidence that Rabin was right? Bear with me, please, as I remind you of those who traveled to Israel on November 6, the day he was laid to rest, to signify their respect for the man and for the peace he had pursued. The United States was represented by President and Mrs. Clinton, by former presidents Ford and Carter, by five members of the Clinton cabinet, by the speaker of the House and its minority leader, by the majority leader of the Senate along with sixteen other senators and diverse other dignitaries. From Jordan, King Hussein and Queen Noor and Crown Prince Hassan, as well as the prime minister and the foreign minister; from Egypt, President Mubarak and the foreign minister; the prime minister of Morocco and senior officials of Mauritania, Oman, Qatar, and Tunisia; the presidents of Albania, Armenia, Azerbaijan, Bulgaria, Estonia, Ethiopia, Finland, France, Germany, Ghana, Italy, Moldova, Norway, Portugal, Romania, Slovenia, Switzerland and Ukraine; the prime ministers of Australia, Belgium, Britain, Canada, the Czech Republic, Denmark, Hungary, Iceland, Ireland, Italy, Latvia, Lithuania, Luxembourg, Malta, the Netherlands, Poland, Russia, Slovakia, South Korea, Spain, Sweden and Turkey; twenty foreign ministers (Armenia, Belarus, Britain, Costa Rica, Cote d'Ivoire, Eritrea, Ethiopia, France, Germany, Guatemala, Italy, Japan, Kazakhstan, Lithuania, Mexico, Norway, Romania, Slovenia, Spain and Ukraine); senior representatives of Argentina, Austria, Brazil, China, Colombia, Congo, Croatia, Cyprus,

Ecuador, Fiji, Greece, India, Jamaica, Kenya, Mongolia, Papua, Singapore, South Africa, Swaziland, Thailand and Yugoslavia; Prince Charles of Britain, Queen Beatrix of the Netherlands and the secretary-general of the United Nations.

Just a dozen years ago—yesterday, really—Israel was neither excoriated nor vilified. It was a full-fledged and even widely admired member of the family of nations. It was neither a convenient cover for anti-Semitism nor a nation state deemed more dangerous than any other.

By itself, the Rabin funeral does not dispose of the "it is 1938" argument. It is possible, for example, that we've since taken a giant step backward, or that 1995 was merely a tiny blip in an otherwise unrelieved story of insult and injury. But it seems to me at the least interesting, and quite possibly important, to ask what happened between 1995 and 2007 to change so dramatically the views of the world as also our own world view, what happened to re-ignite the hatred of others and to extinguish our own rising optimism?

What happened? Oslo crumbled, and Camp David failed. Israel's unilateral withdrawals from South Lebanon and from Gaza didn't accomplish what they were meant to accomplish. The second Intifada happened, Arafat is gone and so, effectively, is Sharon. Hamas's ascendancy happened. More than 25,000 new housing units for Jews in the West Bank happened and the Jewish population of the West Bank grew by 109,000 people. A security fence was begun and is moving towards completion and 9/11 happened. And, arguably most consequential of all, for the last one-third of these nearly twelve years, America has been at war in Iraq, a willful war born of a lie, a war that has caused dismay to our friends and delight to our enemies, a war of terrifying cost in life and limb and treasure and honor, a war that was meant to strike a deadly blow against terrorism but that has, instead, trained up a whole new generation of terrorists, a war, finally, that has damaged America's credibility as a guarantor of the freedom and safety of its allies, including Israel.

More generally, the lesson of these last years is that history is a fickle teacher. Look backward, and there's an ocean of data behind you and no mark to tell you where best to drop your anchor. And just over the horizon, landfall, but if you don't turn and face forward you will not see it.

And that, of course, is the point: those who forget tomorrow are condemned to deny it. Invoking the past to justify the present is the work of fools and knaves; it seeks to substitute nightmares for dreams; it is a diversion from that which properly impels us, the dreams that have sustained our people through all the traumas we have together suffered.

I am not here suggesting that we opt for historical amnesia. I am suggesting, even insisting, that we be ever cautious in our necessarily selective use of history and that among the things we dare not erase is our certainty that, if not *machar* then *machratayim*, if not tomorrow then the next day, a brighter dawn awaits.

Forget that, and opportunity comes and then goes, unrecognized. Forget that, and there would have been no peace treaty between Israel and Egypt, between Israel and Jordan. Yes, it would have been different if they had accepted United Nations resolution 181 in 1947, the partition resolution, and it might have been different if Israel had from the start treated its Arab citizens as Israel's own Declaration of Independence promised it would. It would have been different if the Palestinian resistance had chosen non-violence as its method, it might have been different if there had been three yes's in Khartoum instead of three no's, it would have been different without the occupation and the settlements, it might have been different had the withdrawal from Gaza been mutually agreed to rather than unilaterally undertaken. But what is the point of the blame and the recrimination, save to postpone the work that must eventually be undertaken, the work of reconciliation?

"But," they will say, "there is no partner for that work, there is no partner for peace." True enough, but the peace we say we seek is not, after all, a gift to the others so much as it is a way of ensuring Israel's safety, of liberating it at long last from all the distortions the conflict has bred. There is no partner? Then let us adapt the ancient formula from Pirkei Avot: Where there is no partner, be thou a partner. Not out of weakness nor, for that matter, out of strength, but out of responsibility.

I want to say what that might mean by turning once more to Yitzhak Rabin. There are those who believe that Rabin's turn towards peace was a dramatic departure from the Rabin they thought they knew, from Rabin the fighter, the commander, the consummate military man. In my own view, perhaps only in hindsight, it is a mistake to think that Rabin underwent a profound change. The truly consummate commander knows to make war when war is necessary and to move towards peace when peace is possible. The difference between the Rabin of 1940, when as an eighteen year old he joined the Palmach, and the Rabin of 1948, when he commanded the Harel brigade during Israel's war of independence, and the Rabin of 1967, when he was chief of staff, and the Rabin of 1984 to 1990, when he served as minister of defense, and Rabin's first service as prime minister from 1974 to 1977—between the blunt Rabin of all those years and the Rabin who again became prime minister in 1992, and moved so breathtakingly towards peace, was that the Cold War had ended and with its end, a new window of opportunity was suddenly opened, a window that he knew would not stay open for very long. As Rabin himself said at the peace rally on November 4, 1995, just minutes before he was murdered, "I was a military man for 27 years. I fought so long as there was no chance for peace. I believe that there is now a chance for peace, a great chance." And that was the chance to which his entire life had been a prelude, a new way to defend the Jewish state and to make it secure. This was not a man of war overnight transformed into a man of peace; this was a defender of Israel wise enough to know that changed circumstances enabled, even required, changed strategies. And no strategy so appealed to him, so attracted him, as the strategy of peace.

The window that Rabin saw twelve years ago would, he thought, remain open only so long as Iran was not yet a major power in the region. It now, therefore, appears that window is close to being closed, and not just against Israel but against China and Russia and the United States, against those nations united, against Jordan and Saudi Arabia and others in the region, against the United Nations itself, and Bibi Netanyahu is plain wrong when he says that "no one cares," that "no one says anything."

Ironically, and perhaps precisely because of Iran's rising power, another window now appears to be opening. None of us can say with safety exactly what the Arab League initiative means, but surely the conditional offer for the full normalization of relations with Israel by almost every Arab country—Libya is the only exception—is breathtaking in its potential. Shall that potential not be examined?

It is, of course, possible that in our eagerness for some sort of breakthrough, we may too liberally interpret the proposal's possibilities. Perhaps the initiative, as some observers have suggested, is intended more to embarrass Israel than to promote real change, or perhaps its purposes are internal to the Arab world, a tactical move in the Sunni-Shi'a rivalry. Perhaps the conditions it lays down are simply too far from Israel's priorities to be taken seriously, or perhaps they really amount to a take-it-or-leave-it diktat.

Is all that not worth finding out, finding out not from observers but from the principals? Look how far the initiative is from Khartoum. Look to the specific wording of its clause on Palestinian refugees, which reads as an invitation to negotiation. Or shall Abba Eban's much-quoted line that "the Palestinians never miss an opportunity to miss an opportunity" now perversely come to describe the Jewish state as well?

"Olmert is too weak," they say. "Israel is too preoccupied with corruption," they say. "Islam is too captive to its militants," they say. There are always excuses, and the excuses are not untrue. Diplomacy is the search to snake around the checkpoints built of excuses.

"Ah, but it is 1938," they say. "Checkmate."

Checkmate? But of course it is 1938—and it isn't. It is also 1995—and it isn't. The only certainty is that it *is* 2007, not metaphorically but actually. It is 2007 and next year it will be 2008, and if we do not probe what lies beyond the windows that are open those windows will close and we will have only fetid air to breathe, we will have hung history like a concrete slab around our necks and allowed ourselves to be dragged towards perdition.

Or, more pointedly, shall we who count ourselves lovers of Zion and defenders of Israel persist in the sterile recitation of excuses and rationalizations, continue so vehemently to deny in public that which we readily admit in private? Is that really the best we can offer a troubled Israel, the best we can do on its behalf? Is that what being "pro-Israel" has come to mean?

I began these remarks with the words of a song written some 200 years ago. I close now with some words from another song, this one written more than 3,000 years ago and called Psalm 34: "*Mi ha'ish?*" "What man is he that desires life and loves many days, that he may see good? Keep your tongue from evil and your lips from speaking guile. Depart from evil and do good. Seek peace and pursue it."

3

What is Living and What is Dead in Jewish Twentieth-Century History

Irving Louis Horowitz

Let me start with some concern as to the general themes of this volume, prospects for reliving, or better, avoiding the world of 1938 in 2007; and also specific policies or prospects for a Jewish meeting of Left and Right. It is not that I am immune from or lacking in deep regard over the historic fate of the Jewish people under Nazi totalitarianism, or for that matter, the theological schisms and political differences that inhabit present day Jewish life. That so odious a regime as Nazism, and its malignant present-day advocates, can serve even at this date to weaken and distort Jewish solidarity within American democratic society is certainly reason enough for the general focus of this volume. But the reduction of weighty matters to attractive public relations packages will not create the search for consensus or the solution to problems that drives this period in time; nor will it offset the sense of unease that pervades this paradigm.

I suspect that 1938 was selected as the critical pivotal year in the Nazi behemoth in Germany. After all, the events surrounding Kristallnacht ignited the furies of fascism, and the signs of early resistance or at least awareness on the part of the Jewish communities in many parts of Europe and America. Kristallnacht, also known as "Reichskristallnacht," "Novemberpogrome," "Pogromnacht," "Crystal Night" and the "Night of Broken Glass," was a pogrom against Jews throughout Germany and parts of Austria on November 9 and 10, 1938. Jewish homes and stores were ransacked in a thousand German cities, towns and villages. Ordinary citizens and storm troopers destroyed buildings with sledgehammers, leaving the streets covered in smashed windows. On the "Night of Broken Glass," Jews were beaten to death; it is estimated that over 30,000

Jewish men were taken to concentration camps; and 1,668 synagogues were ransacked or set on fire.

The problem in isolating a single year is that such an emphasis, whatever its symbolic intent, is to shift the problem of Nazi rule and anti-Semitic fervor from a long-term historic process to a singular, albeit tragic event. The seeds of racialism go deep into the German nationalist tradition. The actual start of laws against Jews in a Nazi run state began soon after its coming into power in 1933. Indeed, by 1938, over two thousand measures directed at excluding Jews from normal participation in German civic and political life had been enacted. The gangster marauders that took to the streets of Berlin in 1938 had already been well prepared by a barrage of rules, regulations, laws, propaganda, and systematic ideology enacted by National Socialists. That it took five full years to create mass assaults may well be viewed as a tribute to the passive resistance on the part of some Germans no less than acquiescence and participation on the part of other, and arguably the majority of Germans. Many people also saw that the events of that evening were not an outbreak of the "spontaneous wrath of the German people," as the Nazi propaganda tried to portray it, but as a state-organized act of terror, executed mainly by party activists in casual garb. Kristallnacht as a term criticizing and accusing the Nazi dictatorship within Germany for what took place has largely been forgotten.

To single out 1938 is also to select a year in which the persecution of Jews by the National Socialist regime, occurred at a time in which religious-ethnic cleansing remained largely at the cultural and economic levels. It had not reached the murderous frenzy of Holocaust concentration camp levels. Jews were singled out to be sure, but it was still a period in which some were selectively released from these prison houses of the damned. It was also a period, at least prior to the *Anschluss*, before the border closings, when many Jews were able to migrate to more liberal climates—especially the United States and the United Kingdom, and even France to the West and Russia to the East. In short, 1938 was a bad year for Jewish people, but it was not yet a mass murderous year, and the line between life and death, law and total lawlessness is not one to be crossed lightly; nor was it—even by the Nazis.

Kristallnacht was a defining element in Nazi ideology. It exposed as a sham the Nazi effort to picture Germany as a victim and a peace-loving state. As the meticulous historian John Toland, informed us, it solidified Hitler's belief that the regime had been "too soft," too reticent to pursue the ultra nationalist cause. "The Jew lives and serves his own law but never that of the people or the nation where he has become a citizen. He does not belong to the German people." The xenophobic suspicion of dual national loyalties, like multiple social loyalties in general, has been an anti-Semitic staple of every totalitarian regime—Left as well as Right—in world history.

It is worth recalling that as early as Justin Martyr in the second century after the emergence of the Christian Church, claims were made that God had to provide laws for the Jews "on account of their stubbornness and insubordination" to the one true faith. Thus the argument of Hebraic lawfulness as a natural state of human existence was transformed into a Jewish deviation from the path of love—thus justifying their punishment! In 258, the Bishop of Carthage preached that the destruction of the Temple in 70, and the various Roman assaults on Jews were warranted because Jews suffered from stubbornness and insubordination, and as an ignoble people had forsaken the Messiah. This rhetoric became the standard operating code for physical violence against Jewish persons and possessions, such as the sacking and pillaging that took place in Alexandria in 412. The expulsion and destruction of Jews who failed to convert is not a legacy unique to one nation, nor is it limited or attributable exclusively to the Nazis. Likewise, the pogroms that took place throughout the nineteenth century in Eastern Europe were the product of Russian orthodoxy. This is not an historical exegesis, but a reminder that special "turning points" were in evidence long before 1938. The real issue is why the German-Jewish community, in full knowledge of the history of such oppression, still was divided on the strategy, tactics, and goals of the Hitler regime.

By the start of September 1939, with the Nazi Wehrmacht invasion of Poland, the fate of more than three million Jewish lives was sealed, and it was sealed both by the East as well as the West, by the Soviet-Nazi Non-Aggression Pact and the division of Eastern Europe. This period was marked by expropriation of wealth, deprivation of elementary civil liberties, and finally, ghettoization and mass imprisonment in concentration camps. Such developments were often taken in lockstep of the Nazi invasion of European nations such as Romania, Czechoslovakia, and Hungary. These nations unable to defend themselves were often called upon to identify and yield up their Jewish citizens as the price of survival. The Holocaust timeline properly identifies 1939-1940 as one in which ghettoization was the operative norm, and also in which Western

Democratic states stood quietly by—including the United States which refused an arrangement whereby 70,000 Romanian Jews would be given export visas to this country and to England.

In June 1941, with the invasion of Russia by the German legions, the death knell for another two million Jews living in the Russian sphere under Nazi obligation or sphere of influence was sounded. Under the cover of military actions, the Jewish people were placed in dire jeopardy and harms way. One might well note that without such overt military campaigns beyond the borders of Germany, the events of 1938 inside Germany would have remained a signal warning to the Jewish people, but with such actions, the struggle of national survival took on ominous turns. Dutch became just that, not people of broad liberal Protestant persuasions. Poles who themselves were subject to a loss of three million people or one tenth of the Polish population, saw in their religious differentiation from Jews a chance at survival.

By January 1942, the time of the infamous Wannsee Conference, preparations were institutionalized for the slaughter to come. This was a huge step beyond the Nazi claims that it was interested only in exiling all Jews, and making Germany *Juden frei*. Wannsee became a Draconian response to Western democratic indifference no less than National Socialist determination to once and for all solve the Jewish Question. Reinhard Heydrich, Himmler's second in command of the SS, convened the Wannsee Conference in Berlin with fifteen top National Socialist bureaucrats to coordinate the Final Solution (*Endlösung*) in which the Nazis would attempt to exterminate the entire Jewish population of Europe, an estimated 11 million people. "Europe would be combed of Jews from east to west," Heydrich stated. Wannsee promised and sadly delivered two modes of death: Jews eliminated by hard labor and starvation, known in code language as "natural causes," and "special treatment" or "special actions," execution mostly by gassing.

It was the years of 1942-1945—right up to the very moment the Jewish remnant was liberated by Allied and Red Army troops, which witnessed the maximum horrors of the Holocaust. It was during this final period of the Nazi era that its total fanaticism became evident—not only in law but on the military ground. Even on the verge of Nazi defeat, the crumbling German regime became a world in which priorities shifted from getting troops in and out of battle to bringing Jews to their final destination with a minimum of opposition or disruption. Indeed, the policy aims of the Nazis shifted from winning the war to annihilating the Jewish people—from a "war" that could not be won, to one that could be won.

To ask a rhetorical question as to whether 1938 can be avoided in the United States is itself to open the door to hysteria, to a failure of any appreciation of what this nation is made of—in law, custom, and behavior. It might be wiser to examine those tendencies in the culture—whatever their self-proclamation of ideological intent—that make possible an assault upon Jews as such.

This horrific "timeline" of Nazi aggression is widely known. For that reason, we must pay attention to the sweep of history and system and not the events of a single year. The process of fascist rule, of totalitarianism with the face of racial and religion wrath, is best seen as a struggle against a process, not a reflex action in a moment of time. Otherwise, the capacity to struggle is diminished. We are then reduced to bemoaning the psychological capacity for mass hysteria, but leaving aside the sociological capacity to understand, respond and resist totalitarianism. It is the thirteen-year-long "timeline" of National Socialism, not a singular moment in time that provides the understanding of events long ago. It is that history that may offer an appreciation of events taking place in our time. Analogical reasoning is a risky game; it diminishes the realities of 2007 in world Jewry and serves to resurrect a self-destructive determinist sense of history by conflating it with pre-determined policy.

Political Alignment and the Jewish Question

It needs to be said that the notion of "Left" and "Right" is increasingly not a matter of content but of context. That is to say, the specific substance of what constitutes a liberal or conservative frame of reference is defined less by general principles of rights and obligations, freedom and order, intellect and instinct, etc. than by how such matters connect up with Jewish principles and practices. Having written an essay in 1979 on "Left Fascism" in which I also draw attention to "Right Communism" it should be an apparent absurdity to think that such terms would carry weight in serious present-day discussions of Jewish unity or division at the ideological or political level.

Words such as "Left" and "Right," the tendency to dialectical cleverness, can lead to a belief in false alternatives, in clever polarities that disguise uniform sentiments. In this case, those often take the form of dualism: at one end are those who claim that Jews are just fine as a people—thrifty, intelligent, hard working, philanthropic, and whatnot—but Israel and its people are just distasteful—unkind to their neighbors, intruders in the Middle East, people without civility, aggressive, military minded, and whatnot. There are too many cases to warrant naming names—although one can start with living American ex-presidents as exemplifying such polarized reductionisms. At the other end, are those for whom most recently, like A. B. Yehoshua, simply states that "my identity is an Israeli one and not a Jewish one." In this bizarre scenario, the Jews of the Diaspora, the Jews as such are held responsible for the liquidation of one third of the Jewish people. The Shoah is laid at the doorsteps of the Jewish people themselves, and while Jews the world over deliberate about their continuity as a people, the Israelis are dedicated to solving this issue on a daily basis. In this bizarre scenario, the people of Israel are uniquely endowed with a mission of national existence, at least those with strong biblical values; they are the carriers of the destiny of Jewish civilization.

Just what constitutes "Left" and "Right" in this sort of duality simply defies the imagination. One can find individuals and policymakers of all political persuasions occupying some space on either end or at some intermediary layer of this dichotomization of Israel and the Jews. Within the Jewish forms of religious commitment one can find pious observers declaiming against the state of Israel, as if by its very existence there exists a danger to Jewish survival, while one can likewise come upon those for whom failing to make a commitment to aliyah, to a return to Israel, is no less a sin of major proportions that can result in virtual damnation. What has taken place, in the present no less than the past is what Alvin Rosenfeld most recently called "the failure of Jews to recognize hostility toward them and, in some cases, the willingness of Jews to collude with the agents of such hostility." This theme of the Court Jew is an old story, but variation on this theme is considerable over time and in political and national space.

In some considerable measure, whether one examines commitments to Soviet communism or American capitalism, the tendency has been to tie the Jewish ribbon to a supposedly liberal kite. Thus the continuing and unswerving allegiance of American Jews to the Democratic Party can be viewed as a fixation of belief that Jewish liberation is part and parcel of its universal enterprise. Given the successes of American political economy one can readily explain unswerving Jewish loyalties. Where the issue becomes tacky is how Jewish support for Stalinism was likewise seen not as simply a Left tendency, but as a source of Jewish liberation in particular. The myth of Birodbijan, of a Jewish national homeland locked inside a tyrannical dictatorship became likewise seen as a special way that socialist economies can create egalitarian politics. Alas, in the case of Soviet practice, the myth of Birobidjan unraveled after the close of the

Second World War—leaving the revelations that anti-Semitism was as powerful a guide to Stalinist communism as it was to Nazi socialism.

These tragic outcomes for Jewish people are well documented and need little amplification. What needs emphasis is that painting issues in brush strokes of Left and Right are counterproductive; whereas going further and seeking some cohabitation of Jews within a single political tendency is dialectical day dreaming. Jewish commitments to Jewish survival may be weakened by such phenomena as secularization, inter-marriage, and shifts in commitments from the religious to the political. No less compelling is how these varieties of ideological beliefs lead to a soft landing view of the Israeli condition, of a belief in a bi-national state, in a promotion of the idea of Jewish culpability in everything from atrocities against Palestinians to geographical aggrandizement of adjacent lands. What this creates is the fraying of cohesiveness that is presumably being sought by any ethnic, religious, or national group. As a result, the search for the friends of the Jews and of the Israelis becomes a paradoxical ambition in its own terms.

The issue of healing a breach between Jews on the Left and Jews on the Right has the earmarks of academically inspired cleverness. The concerns of Jews as Jews would remain entirely intact even if one took for granted the solution to differences of opinion say between readers of *Tikkun* and *Commentary*. This is not to deny distinctions between Jewish commitments to the Democratic Party or the lack thereof such a force has to the Republican Party. It is to reduce the issues of moment among Jewish people to a *reductio ad absurdum*—locating Jews on a purely po-litical spectrum warped by failure and mired in certitude. My own belief is that the search for Jewish values as an entity unto themselves can best be located in the terrain of cultural continuity and religion tradition. The sense of law being the source of rewards and punishments rather than men defining rewards and punishments as part of a relativistic cornucopia became an outmoded doctrine in a secular world.

While Jewish commitment to the idea of Zionism is frayed, Chris-tian Zionism has evolved as a "massive and influential movement." These people claim that their views are based on biblical principles and prophesy, supported by both Testaments as a unified document separated more by custom and tradition rather than ethics and theology. They view both the Jewish people and the land of Israel as chosen by God for the purposes of redeeming the world. The passionate devotion to millennial positions, serves to arouse passionate devotion to the Jewish state and a Jewish homeland in the Middle East. Anomalies of this sort abound. These cross-cutting phenomena make damp clay of rigid political concerns as to the nature of both or either Israel as a nation and the Jews as a people.

Protestant evangelicals have been joined by Catholic clerics and lay leadership the world over in the growth of strongly positive views of Jewish theology and tradition alike. One need simply compare the waffling indifference of Pope Pius during the Hitler epoch with the Vatican Councils that emerged after the establishment of the state of Israel, and the realization that earlier forms of religious fanaticism provided the breeding grounds for the Holocaust. The strong sense of Christian identification with its Jewish roots as a positive grounds for association if not reconciliation is not necessarily motivated by dialogues and declarations. Indeed, it is the emergence of Muslim extremism, and its implicit Jihadist declarations against Christian life, not only in the Arab Middle East but no less in the coexistence of faiths in the African sub-Sahara, that changes the equation of contemporary Jewish life from what it was in the age of European totalitarianism.

The Jewish tradition of learning, of the dialectical response, of questioning and answering, itself is a contributory element in the changing character of Judaism in both the Diaspora and in Israel. The haunting specter of dualism is a tradition, which if dogmatically understood can improperly conflate debate with solution, paradoxical formulations for serious problem solving, and appeals to destiny and revelation as the same as the search for policy remedies. It would be foolhardy to expect recognition much less a resolution of this from the combatants. That said, false polarities point up to the need of the Jewish people—wherever they reside, whatever their level of risks, however they look upon each other and those from other persuasions (religious or civic)—for an ideological or theological cease fire, at least when it pertains to issues of survival as a people. If the highest canon in Jewish personal existence is life itself, then the highest canon in Jewish political existence is the life of a people: one people, one faith, and one nation—the last divided between the geographical and the spiritual, but singular nonetheless. Within such a formula, all the battles can rage, outside such a formula, the battles become a menace to survival—of Jews in Israel and of Jews who reside elsewhere.

The larger concern is a search for the grounds of consensus as Jews. That signifies softening the differences between Orthodox, Reform Conservative, Reconstructionist elements in Jewish religious life, doing likewise for the distinction between Ashkenazim and Sephardic strains of Jewish ethnicity, and finding common grounds between Jewish believers who accept the idea of Zionism as a form of national redemption, and those who are less wedded to a particular ideology and prefer to view the Jewish nation as a spiritual entity. Then there are substantial gaps—of Jews both in the Diaspora and in Israel as such, between those who accept the idea of a free capitalist market and those who insist that the state of Israel has a welfare state obligation predicated on socialist norms. Once the discourse is broadened the issue of ideological Left and Right becomes one of several items that require or at least merit the attention of the Jewish people as a whole.

My own formulations lean toward a minimalist approach to resolving issues and conditions that divide Jews. First it is necessary to remain part of the Jewish communion, and second to retain a sense of a Jewish homeland in which Jews need not live but do need to support in times of dire emergency. Eban's approach is deceptive in its minimalism—as it is in art and music. To retain a dedication to the Jewish community whether in religious or cultural terms involves an organizational frame of reference, and not simply verbal presentations. By the same token, commitment to the nation of Israel is more than a faith in the idea of redemption in some remote, undefined future; it entails an appreciation of multiple political loyalties that are cemented by commonalities.

The continuous appeal of Israel is how neatly it fits with the historic and current needs of the United States. In sharing the democratic perspective, in its respect for persons, in its approach to the place of law and morality in defining the limits of national sovereignty and personal behavior alike, the phrase Jewish-American offers a perfect continuum—with tactical differences and policies of the moment notwithstanding, the two nations, culture and traditions can move in tandem. Dare one say at a meeting seeking to unify Jewish patterns of belief, that the Christian-Jewish factor is not simply a divide over the place of Lord Jesus in the Jewish pantheon of belief, but it is also a continuum of inspirational messages and views encoded in the Testaments of the two peoples.

Let it not be forgotten that those who seek the destruction of Israel and the death of Jews are also found to be declaring the destruction of the United States and the death of Christians. In such a world, prospects for a great consensus and coherence within the Jewish people also involve a deeper appreciation of the larger universe that moves in an orbit quite beyond the Jewish condition into the status of free societies and free expression. Our recognition of that worthy fact will bring modesty in our discourse and policy into our search for survival.

The open society historically best served the Jewish culture, whether in medieval Spain, Reformation Holland, Enlightened Germany, imperial England, or industrial United States. It is uniformly the case that illiberal turns of these societies have been worst for the Jews. The Jew is a spiritual as well as material entity, a person who provides global society with an operational set of liberal values, and who in turn fares best in a global society that has a vested, legitimated interest in precisely fostering open ended values for its own thoroughly commonplace Jewish reasons. The open tolerant society however has oftentimes seen the Jew as an enemy of such a society. The French Enlightenment and the European Revolutions of the nineteenth century gave sustenance to the view of the Jew as one step beneath the Christian in holding back the idea of progress, while the Germany and Austria of its own liberal democratic rebellion against authority, saw in the Jew an obstacle to liberation. Indeed, for the Marxian socialist tradition, liberation from Judaism is the only real path open to these people. In point of fact, socialist spokesmen were more punishing in their vision of the Jew than of the Christian—clearly an easier mark in the search for political allies. This special singling out of the Jews made possible the end of lawful behavior for the rest of the world.

If we are to contrast 1938 in Germany and 2007 in the United States, I would note that (a) the existence of the state of Israel is itself a factor absent during the British mandate period; (b) the Holocaust not only took place but is deeply embedded in the spirit and memory of Jews; (c) German-Jewish power was centered in the economy, especially in middle ranges of business, whereas in the United States, Jewish authority, while present in the economy, is most noticeable in the political system and process—and at every level from the federal on down to the local levels; so the level of integration of Jews in American society is far deeper than it was in Nazi Germany; (d) finally, while Jewish numbers may be down at the temple and synagogue levels, it is dramatically higher in the organizational frameworks of Jewish organizational life, from the American Jewish Congress to Hadassah, and throughout college and university life. There are more than 140 Holocaust centers in North America. That in itself is a factor to be reckoned with.

While neither major political party gives direct expression to anti-Semitism and while difference strategies for dealing with terror, armed intervention, and general mobilization exist between the major parties, Jews can readily be found on both sides of the aisle. The marginalization of extremism—Left Communism no less than Right Socialism is so noticeable a difference between the United States today, and Nazi

Germany in the mid-1930s, that it must rank as a critical factor. This is not to say that dangers are illusory. They are very real: Strife between racial and religious groups clearly on the rise, ecological separation of Jews from black and Latino minorities for example is itself a potential powder keg. Jewish divisions between types of religious worship, sexual orientations, and intermarriage as a deepening phenomenon, are far beyond the old European tradition of bifurcation between Ashkenazi and Sephardic ancestors, or even German Jews vs. Russian and Polish Jews. But on larger issues of Jewish survival and Israeli existence there is a broad consensus within the Jewish communities, and between Jews as a whole and the Christian and secular clusters.

If Israel now seems hopelessly out of favor with, even an embarrassment to the developing regions, it may well be because that small nation uniquely combines a political framework of democracy and Jewish culture which accentuates and reinforces a free political environment with a developmental ideology. In its own way, Labor Zionism was a flirtation with socialism that slowly melted away as the European commitment to this ideology softened over time, and became itself a danger to the fragile state of Israeli democracy. Commonplace though it may seem, it must be reaffirmed that whither goes Western democracy, so goes the destiny of the Jewish people. The larger struggles for democracy, however, remain halting and imperfect. Embrace the condition of the world as a whole, and the destiny of the Jewish people in particular. This is not a clash of civilizations; it is a struggle between civilization and barbarism. In recognition of that monumental truth the Jewish people will find its unifying voice and the Israeli nation can refine its mission. Both the Jewish people and the Israeli nation will remain two beams of light that will illumine the path of other peoples and for other nations.

References

Charles Freeman, *The Closing of the Western Mind: The Rise of Faith and the Fall of Reason.* New York: Random House/Vintage Books, 2005, 432 pp. This book, quietly and devastatingly, documents its subject. Along the way, it makes it clear that the persecution and liquidation of Jews is hardly a recent innovation. A recent complement to this work is by Jeremy Cohen, *Christ Killers: The Jews and the Passion from the Bible to the Big Screen.* New York and London: Oxford University Press, 2007. 336 pp. He brings the delicate story of the tensions between faith and reason up to date and into the new media world.

John Toland, *Adolf Hitler* (volume II). New York: Doubleday & Co., 1976. pp. 595-597. These offer the most detailed and authoritative accounts as to Hitler's behavior and ideology as found in the post-war memoirs by Braun, Schacht, and Wiedemann. Given the huge amount of writings on Hitler, it might be simpler and more meaningful to see the common roots of anti-Semitism in its totalitarianism completeness. In this regard, the work of Alan Bullock, *Hitler and Stalin: Parallel Lives*. London: Harper/Collins, 1991, 1189 pp. remains the outstanding historical account of this organic linkage of National Socialism and international communism.

Dan Cohn-Sherbok, *The Politics of Apocalypse: The History and Influence of Christian Zionism*. Oxford: One World Press, 2006, pp. 194-195. Another important work on this issue is by Timothy P. Weber, *On the Road to Armageddon: How Evangelicals Became Israel's Best Friend*. Grand Rapids, Michigan: Baker Academic Publishers, 2004, 336 pp. This serves to round out this complex picture of a new configuration in Jewish–Christian "dialogue."

Alvin Rosenfeld, "Modern Jewish Intellectual Failure: A Brief History" in *The Jewish Divide over Israel: Accusers and Defenders,* edited by Edward Alexander and Paul Bogdanor. New Brunswick and London: Transaction Publishers, 2006, pp. 7-32. There is no better single essay indicating the mythology of Left-Right dichotomies as the source of Jewish dilemmas or solutions; and there are few superior works to this collection that detail the ideological and political divisions in contemporary Jewish life. Perhaps the best predecessor to this work is the essay by the under appreciated Eliezer Berkovits, "The Spiritual Crisis in Israel" written in 1979 and included in *Essential Essays on Judaism*, edited by David Hazony. Jerusalem: Shalem Press, 2002, pp. 201-212.

Compare and contrast the current concerns about Jewish survival by Solomon Goldman, "We Jews: Who Are We and What Should We Do?" in *Midstream*. Volume LIII, No. 1, January-February 2007. pp. 24-27; with those of Hillel Halkin, "If Israel Ceased to Exist", *Commentary*. Volume 123, No. 6, June 2007. pp. 30-35.

Victor Klemperer's trio of books contains the most chilling, clinical and noteworthy accounts of quotidian life in Nazi Germany. *I Shall Bear Witness: 1933-1941*, London: Weidenfeld & Nicholson, 1998, 500 pp. *The Language of the Third Reich*, London: Athlone Press and New Brunswick: Transaction Publishers, 2000, 296 pp. *The Lesser Evil: 1945-1959*, London: Weidenfeld & Nicholson, 2003, 637 pp.

Perhaps the strongest evidence of the enormous shift in attitudes of Christians toward Jews is reflected in the studied passivity of Pope Pius XII toward the Holocaust, in contrast to the intense and deeply personal response of "the Holocaust of the Jewish people" expressed by the late Pope John Paul II (and it should be noted continued by the present Pope Benedict XVI. For comments by and work on Pius XII, see Carol Ritner and John K. Roth, *Pope Pius XII and the Holocaust*, New York: Leicester University Press, 2002, 312 pp.; and Pierre Blet, *Pius XII and the Second World War: According to the Archives of the Vatican,* New York: Paulist Press, 1999. 368 pages. For present day attitudes, see in particular, the personal as well as papal statements made about Auschwitz by John Paul II in *Crossing the Threshold of Hope*, Alfred A. Knopf: New York, 1994, especially pp. 96-99.

Irving Louis Horowitz, "The Legal Processing of Human Rights Violations in Germany and Austria, 1933-1945." *Human Rights Review*. April-June, Volume 6, Number 3, 2005. pp. 119-122. The full documentation of the decrees, laws, regulations and rules limiting and ultimately voiding Jewish rights, is contained in *Das Sonderrecht für die Juden im NS Staat (Eine Sammlung der gesetzlichen Massnahmen und Richtlinien)*, edited by Joseph Walk. Heidelberg: C.F. Muller Verlag, 1996, 452 pp.
[Pre-Pub Text: May 30th, 2007]

4

Can We Choose Politically between Right and Left?

Michael Walzer

One might say: this is an easy question to answer. Between 85 and 90 percent of Jews who voted last November voted for the Democrats, so the people have spoken, as we say, and they have formed a unified and coherent Jewish political front—remarkably unified, given the Jewish capacity for argument and dissent. Back in the Eisenhower years, some 35 percent of Jews voted for the Republicans, now fewer than 15 percent are doing that—we are more and more unified. The choice between right and left has been made, and the choice is for the near-left, the center left, which is a sensible choice, it seems to me; the near-left is where the Jews should be and where most Jews have been, ever since emancipation. We have also provided intellectual support for the far left (and cadres too), but despite the fame of far-left Jews like Trotsky and Rosa Luxemburg, the great majority of Jews have opted, pretty steadily, for a near-left politics. The experience or the memory of hostility and persecution (and the seder rule that requires us to imagine that we ourselves were slaves in Egypt) push us leftwards, and then the far left's rejection of liberalism and pluralism pushes us back toward the center. Self-knowledge as well as self-interest requires us to defend the moral/political world of human rights, civil liberties, and religious toleration.

I believe that the same self-knowledge and self-interest explains Jewish support for the welfare state and for the taxes necessary to sustain it. The old *kehillot* of pre-emancipation days were little welfare states, whose extreme vulnerability made it necessary that every member's resources be available to meet the needs of the community. That recognition, that everything we have isn't simply ours to use as we please, carries over, I think, into the larger world—or, at least, into the larger democratic world, where we are equal citizens, no longer vulnerable in the old ways, but with a good Jewish habit of apprehension.

I doubt, though, that these political choices are what the conference organizers had in mind. They are too easy and too common. The hard questions that confront us today, or that we are meant to confront today, have to do with the standing of Israel in the world and with the necessary defense of Israel by diaspora Jews. How should we respond to the effort, on the left but not only there, to de-legitimize Israeli statehood and sovereignty? Many liberal and leftist Jews are tortured by this question because they hate the occupation and recognize the increasingly difficult, even desperate, situation of the Palestinians in Gaza and the West Bank. Some of these Jews, a small minority, have given up on Israel, deciding that occupation and oppression are virtual entailments of Jewish statehood. I doubt that they can be brought into any unified Jewish political front; we have to regard them as political opponents. (I mean *opponents*, whose arguments we have to address; down the road they may turn out to be enemies, and then we will respond differently, but not yet.) More importantly, right now, most liberal and leftist Jews have not given up on Israel. So what should their (our) political position be?

I will describe that position with five theses or arguments. Since I live on the left and often argue with my neighbors, this is what I believe needs to be said.

1. The Jews are, at one and the same time, a nation and a religious community. The state of Israel is the expression of our nationhood and not of our religion. I know how entangled the two are; nonetheless, we have to work hard to keep them apart, above all, to make sure that the state's coercive power is not used for religious purposes. An American-style separation may not work in Israel, as it wouldn't work in many European nation-states, where religious organizations providing welfare services and education receive significant state support. But that only means that there has to be an Israeli style separation. The important issues have to do with the policies and practices of state institutions—immigration and naturalization, housing and employment discrimination, the appropriate version of multiculturalism in Israeli schools, and so on—but we also have to worry about the use of religious symbols to represent the Jewish nation and its state. As an expression of Jewish nationhood, Israel is exactly as legitimate as any other nation-state: Norway, Bulgaria, or Japan, say—and faces the same moral questions with regard to the resident

members of other nations. We have to insist on this point about nationhood and sovereignty, especially so since most of the people who deny Israel's legitimacy have no quarrel at all with Norway, Bulgaria, or Japan. But as an expression of the Jewish religion, which it is taken to be by many of its critics, though incorrectly, Israel would face more difficult questions, and its legitimacy as a modern democratic state would itself be in question. A Jewish state should not be like, and should not look like, a Catholic or a Muslim state; where one religion is established and its believers hold privileged positions. Hence the importance of separation.

2. The occupation and settlement of Gaza and the West Bank after 1967 was a political and moral mistake of huge dimensions—and it was driven in large part by religious fantasies that should never have figured in political decision-making. It was driven by political fantasies too, no doubt, and there surely were political figures on the right who imagined that they were using religion for their own worldly purposes. But I suspect that messianic Jews who imagined that they were using the secular right for their purposes had a better political sense of what was going on. Now the achievements of their zeal have to be undone—that is the work that Ariel Sharon began, much too late, but wasn't able to finish. Diaspora Jews must support any, every, Israeli politician committed to finishing that task. We should think of withdrawal from the territories as the final step in the creation of a secular Jewish nation-state. We have to hope that it also leads to the creation of a secular Palestinian nation-state—though right now that looks like a long shot.

3. For all the sympathy that liberals and leftists feel, and should feel, for Palestinians in trouble, and they are in deep trouble, it is still necessary to insist that some significant part of their trouble is their own doing. They have produced the worst national liberation movement in the history of national liberation—a movement where there has never been a dominant or even a strong faction committed to the hard practical work of nation-building and prepared to reject the romance of violence and martyrdom. That doesn't excuse Israeli wrongdoing, from the forced removal of Palestinian Arabs in 1948 to the bombing of the Gaza power plant in 2006. I am not interested in making excuses for Israel. We should be critical of Israeli actions whenever criticism is necessary. But we should be critical of Palestinian actions too, and there is a long list of Palestinian actions that require criticism—and rarely receive it on the left today. Here again, there should be no excuses. A left whose members weren't ready to speak out against terrorist attacks, and to name the terrorists and their organizations, would not be a left worth having. And if

we condemn the intrusion of Jewish religious zeal into politics, we have to condemn the intrusion of Islamic zeal at the same time. The political toughness and realism that is supposed to mark the secular left requires also that we recognize the greater power, and therefore the greater danger, of Islamic zeal in the world today.

4. It is often said that Israelis committed to a two-state solution have no partner on the Palestinian side—because of the reiterated endorsement of a terrorist politics in the past; more recently, because of the electoral triumph of Islamic zealots. That may be true, or it may not; it is an empirical question, and it requires an experimental response. You never know if you have a partner until you begin negotiating with the people who might, or might not, turn out to be partners. Israel's leaders should talk to anyone who will talk to them—Syria is an immediate candidate. And they should make concessions to no-one who isn't fully ready to engage in the concession-making business. In the long history of the Exile, the court Jew or the *shtadlan* often had to negotiate with enemies of the Jews, even with vicious anti-Semites, and now, some people seem to think, that's over; we don't do that anymore. What statehood actually means is that we still do it, but from a position of strength that Jews never had before, which Israel has won, at great cost. It isn't shameful to negotiate with one's enemies from a position of strength. That is what *mamlachtiyut*, that's what sovereignty, is for; that's what the Zionist achievement means; that is what statesmen and stateswomen, like Israel's current foreign minister, want to do and should do.

5. Finally, American Jewish liberals and leftists must support the American alliance with Israel. The critique of Israel as an American tool, and of America as an Israeli tool, are both of them examples of ideological silliness—driven by anti-Americanism sometimes, and sometimes by anti-Zionism. Given the willfulness that these two countries so often display, it is surely more realistic to assume that they have wills of their own. They also have their own interests, which can and do come into conflict. But they are allies, and this alliance is crucially important for Israel's security. No Jew who cares about Israel would want it broken, even though many of us are sharply critical of the Bush administration's understanding of what that alliance requires—of America and also of Israel. It would be nice if Israel found other allies in addition to the U.S., and I believe that it has more support in Europe than the European media suggest. But America is crucial, and will be crucial until the Arab world accepts Israel as a state like all the other states in the Middle East (we

may think it's better than all the other states, but they don't have to). There is an old left term for the policy I am advocating: "critical support." We must be both critical and supportive of the American-Israeli alliance.

That is my proposed program for a unified and coherent Jewish political front. Obviously, the right-wing religious Jews who are funding settlement activity on the West Bank won't endorse this program. Nor will left-wing Jews who deny Israel's legitimacy. Every front has its boundaries; political unity is always the unity of some, against others. But this front could be the unity of many. I am not dreaming, like Isaac Babel's Gedalya, of an impossible international. This is a possible politics.

But I have to admit that it rests on the premise that 2007 is not 1938. The policy that I am advocating assumes that American citizenship and Israeli sovereignty have made a difference and make a difference today. It is a Zionist assumption: statehood and citizenship are immensely valuable, and we should be thankful that we have them and that we are not vulnerable in the old ways. I don't doubt the real dangers that Israel confronts, which we have come together in this conference to talk about. But living in fear isn't a necessity now; it is a project—and it is a project that we should reject because it doesn't help us address the dangers we face with the resources we have. Aiming at a unified and coherent political front makes sense. If there were no dangers, or only lesser dangers, we could be as disunited and incoherent as we often long to be. At the same time, we can tolerate wide-ranging disagreements among the members of the front. Tolerating disagreement would not only be a sign of our strength but also of our knowledge of our strength.

In his lovely new book, *Lion's Honey*, a retelling of the Samson story, written before the Lebanon War, David Grossman describes "the well-known Israeli feeling, in the face of any threat that comes along, that the country's security is crumbling…" This feeling, he goes on, "does not reflect one's actual strength, and often carries in its wake an overblown display of force, further complicating the situation. All of this attests, it would seem, to a rather feeble sense of the ownership of the power that has been attained, and, of course, to a deep existential insecurity. This is connected, without a doubt, to the very real dangers lying in wait for Israel, but also to the tragic formative experience of being a stranger in the world, the Jewish sense of not being a nation 'like other nations'…" We all share that sense, and we know the deep insecurity. But we need a clearer recognition of "the power that has been attained" and a calm debate about how to use it.

5

Echoes of 1938

Alan Dershowitz

The theme is 1938 and I agree with my colleagues that this is not 1938. Israel is a powerful country able to defend itself. The Jews of America are influential—not, as in the view of some, like Jimmy Carter, *too* influential—but we certainly do have our ability to influence policy in ways that were not possible in 1938.

I do, however, want to discuss one way in which I hear echoes of 1938. I refer to something happening today on the hard left and in some respects on the hard right—but I think we're more focused on the hard left because the hard left is more influential today on college and university campuses and in Europe. What is happening on the hard left is not only extreme criticism of Israel, along with attempts to de-legitimate the Jewish State and Zionism, but something far, far worse. What we are really seeing, for the first time, is a dehumanization of Israel, a dehumanization of Israelis and a dehumanization of Jewish supporters of Israel, and I do not mean only Jewish supporters on the hard right. I mean to include in the dehumanization even people like myself and Michael Walzer, who is a liberal political philosopher at Princeton. This dehumanization can be heard if one listens to people like Noam Chomsky and Norman Finkelstein, who are extraordinarily influential on college campuses today, appearing regularly on programs like *Democracy Now* and writing regularly for *CounterPunch*. They go much further than simply de-legitimating Israel.

This characterizes the debate on college campuses today in the U.S. and in Europe. I recently came back from a tour of many European campuses. The anti-Israel criticism there is not about whether or not the occupation should end. It is not about Israeli policy. It is a vicious attempt simply to dehumanize Israel. It is, in fact, far worse today than anything that was ever directed against South Africa during the worst days of apartheid, anything directed against China for its occupation of Tibet, worse than anything directed against the Sudan, worse than anything directed against North Korea and Iran. With all of these other cases, there was a debate. It may have been an extreme debate but it was a debate. On college campuses today, however, one finds simply the hurling of phrases like "Nazism" and "Fascism." There is almost no opportunity to have nuanced and reasonable debate.

Take, for example, a letter I received from a very distinguished professor at Rutgers named Robert Trivers. He called me a rancid defender of Israeli fascism, talked about mini-holocausts that are being conducted by Israel and ends his letter by saying that I should look forward to a visit from him, because "Nazis and neo-Nazis and apologists such as yourself need to be confronted directly." I get threats all the time—threats on my life, threats on my family, threats on my health—because I am a rational, moderate defender of Israel and I have long been opposed to the occupation. I favor a two-state solution. I favor the Camp David and Taba Accords. My books have been supported by people like Amos Oz. And yet, I am constantly referred to as a Nazi and a neo-Nazi and fascist. In Europe, my position is referred to as a neo-conservative position. Actually, though, it is a liberal position. Indeed, it is very important that supporters of Israel continue to listen very carefully to Israel's liberal critics, and specifically to know the difference between critical friends and unthinking enemies. We cannot abandon the left. We may have been abandoned by the hard left, by the Chomskys and the Finkelsteins and the Tony Judts and others, but we must not use that as an excuse for turning right. I think that Israel has to be supported by the moderate mainstream left and right. Those of us like the political philosopher Michael Walzer and myself, who live on the left—he more on the left, me more on the center left—have to devote ourselves and our efforts to building a coalition for Israel that includes mainstream and moderate liberals.

It is, therefore, critical to focus on college campuses because I think the dehumanization effort I have been describing has a very clear goal. The goal is to influence the attitudes of the future leaders of America. The support of the U.S. remains crucial. We can, today, take for granted essentially the support of people in our generation – our age group – the support of mainstream voters. But we cannot take for granted continuing support of Israel by my students and those of my colleagues. These are people who in twenty years will be the presidents of the United States, the senators, the congressmen, the media leaders, the business leaders. And there is a real effort not only to de-legitimize Israel among these people but to dehumanize the supporters of Israel and to transform them into the kind of caricatures that I see on cartoons today in Europe and all over the world, cartoons which show Israelis as monsters, dehumanized. There are pictures there of Palestinian children put in meat boxes and slaughtered by a horrible and brutal Israeli.

It is, in fact, so difficult to get a debate going on college campuses today, even about the very issues that many liberal critics of Israel would like to see us debate. It is so hard to get a debate going about the occupation, for example, because immediately it is met by these dehumanizing claims of fascism and the like. I am an eyewitness to that phenomenon.

Nevertheless, where I disagree with some of my fellow liberal commentators on Israel is that I think that nothing Israel does today will have any major impact on the far left, those who dehumanize. I think we should urge Israel to end the occupation, to try to make peace, to do all the things that its liberal critics have been suggesting. But I do not think there are any assurances that Israeli actions will have a major impact on the kind of hard left opposition to Israel, nor on the kind of media opposition as reflected, for example, by the recent boycott of a union of British journalists. Consider the historical dynamics, and what occurred precisely when Israel offered to make a very generous peace settlement at Camp David and Taba—95 to 97 percent of the West Bank, all of the Gaza strip, a Palestinian capital in Jerusalem, a $35 billion refugee package—however you characterize it, it was an extraordinarily generous offer. Arafat, by accepting it, could have established a Palestinian state. And yet it was almost precisely at that point that international and media attention and opinion started turning ferociously against Israel. When Israel has made efforts towards peace, there has been no sense of any change in attitudes. Whatever Israel does, in fact, is mischaracterized by the hard left.

So those of us who support Israel and who support moderate resolutions to the conflict—a two-state solution and an end to the occupation —have to focus much more of our attention on making what I call the 90 percent case for Israel, not the 100 percent case for Israel. The reason that I think Americans who support Israel can make a better case than the Israeli government is that the Israeli government, through its diplomats, inevitably has to make the 100 percent case, the case reflected in today's *New York Times* by the story of how the settlers in Hebron feel emboldened, seizing on the weakness of the current Israeli government to strengthen their positions and to strengthen the occupation. I feel no obligation to defend that aspect of Israeli policy. What's important, then, is to make the case, the case that American liberals and Israeli leftists like Amos Oz can make, the case that I and other liberal observers can make, a case for Zionism, a case for a peaceful resolution of the Middle East conflict, but a case that does not require us to support every single aspect of Israeli policy.

Nevertheless, it is not clear to me that what Israel does will have a major impact on college campuses. The ignorance of the debate on college campuses today is rampant. And again, I am an eyewitness. I probably speak on more college campuses than nearly anybody, and when I speak on college campuses, I find it so hard to engage intelligently with opponents of Israel. After visiting college campuses, it is almost a relief to read Jimmy Carter because Jimmy Carter and Stephen Walt and John Mearsheimer and Tony Judt at least have something to talk about, something to debate about. And the interesting thing is that the attitudes of Judt and Walt and Mearsheimer and Carter, attitudes which condemn American lobbying groups toward Israel, attitudes which oppose the two-state solution, are today regarded as moderate on college campuses. And the two-state solution, the end of the occupation, the positions taken by myself and many other liberal critics of Israel, are regarded today as neo-Fascist and hard, hard right positions.

So, am I optimistic? I am optimistic in the sense that I think Israel is in a strong position and the American Jewish community is in a strong position. But I am not optimistic for the future unless we see some significant changes. In particular, unless we can incorporate within the pro-Israel community and within the case for Israel the views of our critical friends —Princeton's Michael Walzer, for example, and others like him—I think we are in danger of losing the moderate left. And it will always be wrong for Israel to become a right-left issue, a Republican-Democrat issue, a Bush versus whoever his opponent is issue. We must honor support for Israel everywhere in the mainstream, on the mainstream left and on the mainstream right.

The hard left is already lost. Just take a look, for example, at the faculty at Columbia University, the Middle East Studies Department, or the faculty at DePaul University, which just voted, by a count of nine to three, to give Norman Finkelstein tenure despite the fact that Finkelstein has never produced any kind of scholarship other than ad hominem attacks.

The person who brought Norman Finkelstein to DePaul is a woman who is a follower of Farrakhan and an anti-Semite. The Middle East studies departments of dozens of universities around the U.S. are virulently anti-Israel, engage in the kind of dehumanizing that I have discussed here, and impose their views on students. The amount of ignorant teaching that goes on in universities today, one-sided ignorant teaching, is rampant, and is reflected in the way some students are terrified of taking courses with teachers like this. Norman Finkelstein, for example, was thrown out of Brooklyn College, Hunter College and other colleges because he abused students with views different from his own and you see this kind of thing going on all over the place.

I think that students are open-minded, for the most part, and when I speak on college campuses, I try to speak directly to moderate students, to the future leaders. I try to use their professors essentially against them, using their professors as exhibits showing them how often their extremist professors are not only ignorantly anti-Israel but ignorantly anti-American, ignorantly anti-Western, ignorantly favorable to views that are so antagonistic to modern, secular and liberal values. The propaganda that is expressed by some faculty members today is just unbelievable. I am, however, optimistic about the students and I find that after I speak, I get emails from students saying: "We didn't know. We just didn't know."

There is so much ignorance about the history of the conflict, ignorance about the 1967 war, for example, and about the 1948 war—a case in which some critics go over the line and use the term "ethnic cleansing" to describe what happened to the Palestinian refugees during that time. It is so much more complicated than that. There has never been a weaker claim of refugee status than the Palestinian claim. Had the Palestinians and the Arabs not started the 1948 war, Israel would have accepted —with difficulty—but accepted a significant Palestinian population. Every other community of refugees post-World War II has managed to integrate into their host population. Similarly, after the 1967 war, Israeli General Moshe Dayan made it very clear that he was waiting for the phone call, prepared to give back the West Bank if Jordan would make peace. Instead, Jordan disassociated itself from the West Bank. As you know, there were efforts by Israel to give back the Gaza strip to Egypt during the early Camp David negotiations.

I do think it is important to put all this in historical context. I do agree with Israel's liberal critics that many mistakes were made and that in the exuberance of post-'67, there were things that should have been done that were not done. But again I would join some of those same critics in saying that so much of the fault lies with the Palestinians as well. They could today have been celebrating their fifth or sixth anniversary of statehood on the vast majority of the West Bank and all of Gaza if they wanted a two-state solution more than they wanted the destruction of Israel. And we do not hear often enough what I think is so centrally important: that the Palestinian leadership today does not want a two-state solution. It wants a one-state solution. Tony Judt wants a one-state solution. A one-state solution is not an alternative for Israel. It is an alternative *to* Israel. And I think it is so important that we put a large part of the blame for the current situation on the unwillingness of Palestinians, at least the majority of Palestinians, to take 90 percent of a loaf rather than 200 percent of a loaf.

There is, of course, much blame to go around. But I think in making the moderate case for Israel, one should not exaggerate Israel's faults. One should not blame everything on the occupation. Continuing terrorism and the refusal of the Palestinians to accept a two-state solution play at least as much of a role as the occupation, and the occupation itself has to be understood in context. That is the past. The future is that Israel has no role to play in continuing to occupy large Palestinian population centers. True, territorial adjustments must be made in the interest of peace and in the interest of reality. But the two-state solution with Israel leaving the vast majority of the West Bank, as it has the Gaza strip, is the way of the future. It has to be done. Still, I am not sure it will improve Israel's position in the campus debate or elsewhere. Israel wants to see land for peace. What they are getting instead is land for rocket launching, land for kidnapping, land for terrorism. And so the international community has to assure Israel that if it does give back land, it will get peace instead of increasingly effective terrorism directed at civilian populations.

6

The Case for Bombing Iran

Norman Podhoretz

Although many persist in denying it, I continue to believe that what September 11, 2001 did was to plunge us headlong into nothing less than another world war. I call this new war World War IV, because I also believe that what is generally known as the cold war was actually World War III, and that this one bears a closer resemblance to that great conflict than it does to World War II. Like the cold war, as the military historian Eliot Cohen was the first to recognize, the one we are now in has ideological roots, pitting us against Islamofascism, yet another mutation of the totalitarian disease we defeated first in the shape of Nazism and fascism and then in the shape of Communism; it is global in scope; it is being fought with a variety of weapons, not all of them military; and it is likely to go on for decades.

What follows from this way of looking at the last five years is that the military campaigns in Afghanistan and Iraq cannot be understood if they are regarded as self-contained wars in their own right. Instead we have to see them as fronts or theaters that have been opened up in the early stages of a protracted global struggle. The same thing is true of Iran. As the currently main center of the Islamofascist ideology against which we have been fighting since 9/11, and as (according to the State Department's latest annual report on the subject) the main sponsor of the terrorism that is Islamofascism's weapon of choice, Iran too is a front in World War IV. Moreover, its effort to build a nuclear arsenal makes it the potentially most dangerous one of all.

The Iranians, of course, never cease denying that they intend to build a nuclear arsenal, and yet in the same breath they openly tell us what they intend to do with it. Their first priority, as repeatedly and unequivocally announced by their president, Mahmoud Ahmadinejad, is to "wipe Israel off the map," a feat that could not be accomplished by conventional weapons alone.

But Ahmadinejad's ambitions are not confined to the destruction of Israel. He also wishes to dominate the greater Middle East, and thereby to control the oilfields of the region and the flow of oil out of it through the Persian Gulf. If he acquired a nuclear capability, he would not even have to use it in order to put all this within his reach. Intimidation and blackmail by themselves would do the trick.

Nor are Ahmadinejad's ambitions merely regional in scope. He has a larger dream of extending the power and influence of Islam throughout Europe, and this too he hopes to accomplish by playing on the fear that resistance to Iran would lead to a nuclear war. And then, finally, comes the largest dream of all: what Ahmadinejad does not shrink from describing as "a world without America." Demented though he may be, I doubt that Ahmadinejad is so crazy as to imagine that he could wipe America off the map even if he had nuclear weapons. But what he probably does envisage is a diminution of the American will to oppose him: that is, if not a world without America, he will settle, at least in the short run, for a world without much American influence.

Not surprisingly, the old American foreign policy establishment and many others say that these dreams are nothing more than the fantasies of a madman. They also dismiss those who think otherwise as neoconservative alarmists trying to drag this country into another senseless war that is in the interest not of the United States but only of Israel. But the irony is that Ahmadinejad's dreams are more realistic than the dismissal of those dreams as merely insane delusions. To understand why, an analogy with World War III may help.

At certain points in that earlier war, some of us feared that the Soviets might seize control of the oil fields of the Middle East, and that the West, faced with a choice between surrendering to their dominance or trying to stop them at the risk of a nuclear exchange, would choose surrender. In that case, we thought, the result would be what in those days went by the name of Finlandization.

In Europe, where there were large Communist parties, Finlandization would take the form of bringing these parties to power so that they could establish "Red Vichy" regimes like the one already in place in Finland, regimes whose subservience to the Soviet will in all things, domestic and foreign alike, would make military occupation unnecessary and would therefore preserve a minimal degree of national independence.

In the United States, where there was no Communist party to speak of, we speculated that Finlandization would take a subtler form. In the realm of foreign affairs, politicians and pundits would arise to celebrate the arrival of a new era of peace and friendship in which the Cold War policy of containment would be scrapped, thus giving the Soviets complete freedom to expand without encountering any significant obstacles. And in the realm of domestic affairs, Finlandization would mean that the only candidates running for office with a prayer of being elected would be those who promised to work toward a sociopolitical system more in harmony with the Soviet model than the unjust capitalist plutocracy under which we had been living.

Of course, by the grace of God, the dissidents behind the Iron Curtain, and Ronald Reagan, we won World War III and were therefore spared the depredations that Finlandization would have brought. Alas, we are far from knowing what the outcome of World War IV will be. But in the meantime, looking at Europe today, we already see the unfolding of a process analogous to Finlandization: it has been called, rightly, Islamization. Consider, for example, what happened when, only a few weeks ago, the Iranians captured fifteen British sailors and marines and held them hostage. Did the Royal Navy, which once boasted that it ruled the waves, immediately retaliate against this blatant act of aggression, or even threaten to do so unless the captives were immediately released? Not by any stretch of the imagination. Indeed, using force was the last thing in the world the British contemplated doing, as they made sure to announce. Instead they relied on the "soft power" so beloved of "sophisticated" Europeans and their American fellow travelers.

But then, as if this show of impotence were not humiliating enough, the British were unable even to mobilize any of that soft power. The European Union, of which they are a member, turned down their request to threaten Iran with a freeze of imports. As for the UN, under whose very auspices they were patrolling the international waters in which the sailors were kidnapped, it once again showed its true colors by refusing even to condemn the Iranians. The most the Security Council could bring itself to do was to express "grave concern." Meanwhile, a member of the British cabinet was going the Security Council one better. While registering no objection to propaganda pictures of the one woman hostage, who had been forced to shed her uniform and dress for the cameras in Muslim clothing, Health Secretary Patricia Hewitt pronounced it "deplorable" that she should have permitted herself to be photographed with a cigarette in her mouth. "This," said Hewitt, "sends completely the wrong message to our young people."

According to John Bolton, our former ambassador to the UN, the Iranians were testing the British to see if there would be any price to pay for committing what would once have been considered an act of war. Having received his answer, Ahmadinejad could now reap the additional benefit of, as the British commentator Daniel Johnson puts it, "posing as a benefactor" by releasing the hostages, even while ordering more attacks in Iraq and even while continuing to arm terrorist organizations, whether Shiite (Hizballah) or Sunni (Hamas). For fanatical Shiites though Ahmadinejad and his ilk assuredly are, they are obviously willing to set sectarian differences aside when it comes to forging jihadist alliances against the infidels.

If, then, under present circumstances Ahmadinejad could bring about the extraordinary degree of kowtowing that resulted from the kidnapping of the British sailors, what might he not accomplish with a nuclear arsenal behind him, nuclear bombs that could be fitted on missiles capable of reaching Europe? As to such a capability, Robert G. Joseph, the U.S. Special Envoy for Nuclear Non-Proliferation, tells us that Iran is "expanding what is already the largest offensive missile force in the region. Moreover, it is reported to be working closely with North Korea, the world's number-one missile proliferator, to develop even more capable ballistic missiles." This, Joseph goes on, is why "analysts agree that in the foreseeable future Iran will be armed with medium- and long-range ballistic missiles," and it is also why "we could wake up one morning to find that Iran is holding Berlin, Paris or London hostage to whatever its demands are then."

As with Finlandization, Islamization extends to the domestic realm, too. In one recent illustration of this process, as reported in the British press, "schools in England are dropping the Holocaust from history lessons to avoid offending Muslim pupils...whose beliefs include Holocaust denial." But this is an equal-opportunity capitulation, since the schools are also eliminating lessons about the Crusades because "such lessons often contradict what is taught in local mosques."

But why single out England? If anything, much more, and worse, has been going on in other European countries, including France, Germany, Italy, Spain, Denmark, and the Netherlands. All of these countries have large and growing Muslim populations demanding that their religious values and sensibilities be accommodated at the expense of the traditional values of the West, and even in some instances of the law. Yet rather than insisting that, like all immigrant groups before them, they assimilate to Western norms, almost all European politicians have been cravenly giving in to the Muslims' outrageous demands.

As in the realm of foreign affairs, if this much can be accomplished under present circumstances, what might not be done if the process were being backed by Iranian nuclear blackmail? Already some observers are warning that by the end of the twenty-first century the whole of Europe will be transformed into a place to which they give the name Eurabia. Whatever chance there may still be of heading off this eventuality would surely be lessened by the menacing shadow of an Iran armed with nuclear weapons, and only too ready to put them into the hands of the terrorist groups to whom it is even now supplying rockets and other explosive devices.

And the United States? As would have been the case with Finlandization, we would experience a milder form of Islamization here at home. But not in the area of foreign policy. Like the Europeans, confronted by Islamofascists armed by Iran with nuclear weapons, we would become more and more hesitant to risk resisting the emergence of a world shaped by their will and tailored to their wishes. For even if Ahmadinejad did not yet have missiles with a long enough range to hit the United States, he would certainly be able to unleash a wave of nuclear terror against us. If he did, he would in all likelihood act through proxies, for whom he would with characteristic brazenness disclaim any responsibility even if the weapons used by the terrorists were to bear telltale markings identifying them as of Iranian origin. At the same time, the opponents of retaliation and other antiwar forces would rush to point out that there was good reason to accept this disclaimer and, markings or no markings (could they not have been forged?), no really solid evidence to refute it.

In any event, in these same centers of opinion, such a scenario is regarded as utter nonsense. In their view, none of the things it envisages would follow even if Ahmadinejad should get the bomb, because the fear of retaliation would deter him from attacking us just as it deterred the Soviets in World War III. For our part, moreover, the knowledge that we were safe from attack would preclude any danger of our falling into anything like Islamization.

But listen to what Bernard Lewis, the greatest authority of our time on the Islamic world, has to say in this context on the subject of deterrence:

MAD, mutual assured destruction, [was effective] right through the cold war. Both sides had nuclear weapons. Neither side used them, because both sides knew the other would retaliate in kind. This will not work with a religious fanatic [like Ahmadinejad]. For him, mutual assured destruction is not a deterrent, it is an inducement. We know already that [Iran's leaders] do not give a damn about killing their own people in great numbers. We have seen it again and again. In the final scenario, and this applies all the more strongly if they kill large numbers of their own people, they are doing them a favor. They are giving them a quick free pass to heaven and all its delights.

Nor are they inhibited by a love of country:

We do not worship Iran, we worship Allah. For patriotism is another name for paganism. I say let this land [Iran] burn. I say let this land go up in smoke, provided Islam emerges triumphant in the rest of the world.

These were the words of the Ayatollah Khomeini, who ruled Iran from 1979 to 1989, and there is no reason to suppose that his disciple Ahmadinejad feels any differently.

Still less would deterrence work where Israel was concerned. For as the Ayatollah Rafsanjani (who is supposedly a "pragmatic conservative") has declared:

If a day comes when the world of Islam is duly equipped with the arms Israel has in possession...application of an atomic bomb would not leave anything in Israel, but the same thing would just produce damages in the Muslim world.

In other words, Israel would be destroyed in a nuclear exchange, but Iran would survive.

In spite of all this, we keep hearing that all would be well if only we agree—in the currently fashionable lingo—to "engage" with Iran, and that even if the worst came to the worst we could—to revert to the same lingo—"live" with a nuclear Iran. It is when such things are being said that, alongside the resemblance between now and World War III, a parallel also becomes evident between now and the eve of World War II.

By 1938, Germany under Adolf Hitler had for some years been rearming in defiance of its obligations under the Versailles treaty and other international agreements. Yet even though Hitler in Mein Kampf had explicitly spelled out the goals he was now preparing to pursue, scarcely anyone took him seriously. To the imminent victims of the war he was soon to start, Hitler's book and his inflammatory speeches were nothing more than braggadocio or, to use the more colorful word Hannah Arendt once applied to Adolf Eichmann, rodomontade: the kind of red meat any politician might throw to his constituents at home. Hitler might sound at times like a madman, but in reality he was a shrewd operator with whom one could—in the notorious term coined by the London Times—"do business." The business that was done under this assumption was the Munich Agreement of 1938, which the British Prime Minister Neville Chamberlain declared had brought "peace in our time."

It was thanks to Munich that "appeasement" became one of the dirtiest words in the whole of our political vocabulary. Yet appeasement had always been an important and entirely respectable tool of diplomacy, signifying the avoidance of war through the alleviation of the other side's grievances. If Hitler had been what his eventual victims imagined he was, that is, a conventional statesman pursuing limited aims and using the threat of war only as a way of strengthening his bargaining position, it would indeed have been possible to appease him and thereby to head off the outbreak of another war.

But Hitler was not a conventional statesman and, although for tactical reasons he would sometimes pretend otherwise, he did not have limited aims. He was a revolutionary seeking to overturn the going international system and to replace it with a new order dominated by Germany, which also meant the political culture of Nazism. As such, he offered only two choices: resistance or submission. Finding this reality unbearable, the world persuaded itself that there was a way out, a third alternative, in negotiations. But given Hitler's objectives, and his barely concealed lust for war, negotiating with him could not conceivably have led to peace. It could have had only one outcome, which was to buy him more time to start a war under more favorable conditions. As most historians now agree, if he had been taken at his own word about his true intentions, he could have been stopped earlier and defeated at an infinitely lower cost.

Which brings us back to Ahmadinejad. Like Hitler, he is a revolutionary whose objective is to overturn the going international system and to replace it in the fullness of time with a new order dominated by Iran and ruled by the religio-political culture of Islamofascism. Like Hitler, too, he is entirely open about his intentions, although, again like Hitler, he sometimes pretends that he wants nothing more than his country's just due. In the case of Hitler in 1938, this pretense took the form of claiming that no further demands would be made if sovereignty over the Sudetenland were transferred from Czechoslovakia to Germany. In the case of Ahmadinejad, the pretense takes the form of claiming that Iran is building nuclear facilities only for peaceful purposes and not for the production of bombs.

But here we come upon an interesting difference between then and now. Whereas in the late 1930s almost everyone believed, or talked himself into believing, that Hitler was telling the truth when he said he had no further demands to make after Munich, no one believes that Ahmadinejad is telling the truth when he says that Iran has no wish to develop a nuclear arsenal. In addition, virtually everyone agrees that it would be best if he were stopped, only not, God forbid, with military force, not now, and not ever.

But if military force is ruled out, what is supposed to do the job?

Well, to begin with, there is that good old standby, diplomacy. And so, for three-and-a-half years, even pre-dating the accession of Ahmadinejad to the presidency, the diplomatic gavotte has been danced with Iran, in negotiations whose carrot-and-stick details no one can remember, not even, I suspect, the parties involved. But since, to say it again, Ahmadinejad is a revolutionary with unlimited aims and not a statesman with whom we can "do business," all this negotiating has had the same result as Munich had with Hitler. That is, it has bought the Iranians more time in which they have moved closer and closer to developing nuclear weapons.

Then there are sanctions. As it happens, sanctions have very rarely worked in the past. Worse yet, they have usually ended up hurting the hapless people of the targeted country while leaving the leadership unscathed. Nevertheless, much hope has been invested in them as a way of bringing Ahmadinejad to heel. Yet thanks to the resistance of Russia and China, both of which have reasons of their own to go easy on Iran, it has proved enormously difficult for the Security Council to impose sanctions that could even conceivably be effective. At first, the only measures to which Russia and China would agree were much too limited even to bite. Then, as Iran continued to defy Security Council resolutions and to block inspections by the International Atomic Energy Agency (IAEA) that it was bound by treaty to permit, not even the Russians and the Chinese were able to hold out against stronger sanctions. Once more, however, these have had little or no effect on the progress Iran is making toward the development of a nuclear arsenal. On the contrary: they, too, have bought the Iranians additional time in which to move ahead.

Since hope springs eternal, some now believe that the answer lies in more punishing sanctions. This time, however, their purpose would be not to force Iran into compliance, but to provoke an internal uprising against Ahmadinejad and the regime as a whole. Those who advocate this course tell us that the "mullocracy" is very unpopular, especially with young people, who make up a majority of Iran's population. They tell us that these young people would like nothing better than to get rid of the oppressive and repressive and corrupt regime under which they now live and to replace it with a democratic system. And they tell us, finally, that if Iran were so transformed, we would have nothing to fear from it even if it were to acquire nuclear weapons.

Once upon a time, under the influence of Bernard Lewis and others I respect, I too subscribed to this school of thought. But after three years and more of waiting for the insurrection they assured us back then was on the verge of erupting, I have lost confidence in their prediction. Some of them blame the Bush administration for not doing enough to encourage an uprising, which is why they have now transferred their hopes to sanctions that would inflict so much damage on the Iranian economy that the entire populace would rise up against the rulers. Yet whether or not this might happen under such circumstances, there is simply no chance of getting Russia and China, or the Europeans for that matter, to agree to the kind of sanctions that are the necessary precondition.

At the outset, I stipulated that the weapons with which we are fighting World War IV are not all military, that they also include economic, diplomatic, and other nonmilitary instruments of power. In exerting pressure for reform on countries like Egypt and Saudi Arabia, these nonmilitary instruments are the right ones to use. But it should be clear by now to any observer not in denial that Iran is not such a country. As we know from Iran's defiance of the Security Council and the IAEA even while the United States has been warning Ahmadinejad that "all options" remain on the table, ultimatums and threats of force can no more stop him than negotiations and sanctions have managed to do. Like them, all they accomplish is to buy him more time.

In short, the plain and brutal truth is that if Iran is to be prevented from developing a nuclear arsenal, there is no alternative to the actual use of military force, any more than there was an alternative to force if Hitler was to be stopped in 1938.

Since a ground invasion of Iran must be ruled out for many different reasons, the job would have to be done, if it is to be done at all, by a campaign of air strikes. Furthermore, because Iran's nuclear facilities are dispersed, and because some of them are underground, many sorties and bunker-busting munitions would be required. And because such a campaign is beyond the capabilities of Israel, and the will, let alone the courage, of any of our other allies, it could be carried out only by the United States.* Even then, we would probably be unable to get at all the

---

* However, a new study by two members of the Security Studies Program at MIT concludes that the Israeli Air Force "now possesses the capability to destroy even well-hardened targets in Iran with some degree of confidence." The problem is that all of the many contingencies involved would have to go right for such a mission to succeed.

underground facilities, which means that, if Iran were still intent on going nuclear, it would not have to start over again from scratch. But a bombing campaign would without question set back its nuclear program for years to come, and might even lead to the overthrow of the mullahs.

The opponents of bombing—not just the usual suspects but many both here and in Israel who have no illusions about the nature and intentions and potential capabilities of the Iranian regime—disagree that it might end in the overthrow of the mullocracy. On the contrary, they are certain that all Iranians, even the democratic dissidents, would be impelled to rally around the flag. And this is only one of the worst-case scenarios they envisage. To wit: Iran would retaliate by increasing the trouble it is already making for us in Iraq. It would attack Israel with missiles armed with non-nuclear warheads but possibly containing biological and/or chemical weapons. There would be a vast increase in the price of oil, with catastrophic consequences for every economy in the world, very much including our own. The worldwide outcry against the inevitable civilian casualties would make the anti-Americanism of today look like a love-fest.

I readily admit that it would be foolish to discount any or all of these scenarios. Each of them is, alas, only too plausible. Nevertheless, there is a good response to them, and it is the one given by John McCain. The only thing worse than bombing Iran, McCain has declared, is allowing Iran to get the bomb.

And yet those of us who agree with McCain are left with the question of whether there is still time. If we believe the Iranians, the answer is no. In early April, at Iran's Nuclear Day festivities, Ahmadinejad announced that the point of no return in the nuclearization process had been reached. If this is true, it means that Iran is only a small step away from producing nuclear weapons. But even supposing that Ahmadinejad is bluffing, in order to convince the world that it is already too late to stop him, how long will it take before he actually turns out to have a winning hand?

If we believe the CIA, perhaps as much as ten years. But CIA estimates have so often been wrong that they are hardly more credible than the boasts of Ahmadinejad. Other estimates by other experts fall within the range of a few months to six years. Which is to say that no one really knows. And because no one really knows, the only prudent—indeed, the only responsible—course is to assume that Ahmadinejad may not be bluffing, or may only be exaggerating a bit, and to strike at him as soon as it is logistically possible.

In his 2002 State of the Union address, President Bush made a promise:

> We'll be deliberate, yet time is not on our side. I will not wait on events, while dangers gather. I will not stand by, as peril draws closer and closer. The United States of America will not permit the world's most dangerous regimes to threaten us with the world's most destructive weapons.

In that speech, the president was referring to Iraq, but he has made it clear on a number of subsequent occasions that the same principle applies to Iran. Indeed, he has gone so far as to say that if we permit Iran to build a nuclear arsenal, people fifty years from now will look back and wonder how we of this generation could have allowed such a thing to happen, and they will rightly judge us as harshly as we today judge the British and the French for what they did and what they failed to do at Munich in 1938. I find it hard to understand why George W. Bush would have put himself so squarely in the dock of history on this issue if he were resigned to leaving office with Iran in possession of nuclear weapons, or with the ability to build them. Accordingly, my guess is that he intends, within the next twenty-one months, to order air strikes against the Iranian nuclear facilities from the three U.S. aircraft carriers already sitting nearby.

But if that is what he has in mind, why is he spending all this time doing the diplomatic dance and wasting so much energy on getting the Russians and the Chinese to sign on to sanctions? The reason, I suspect, is that—to borrow a phrase from Robert Kagan—he has been "giving futility its chance." Not that this is necessarily a cynical ploy. For it may well be that he has entertained the remote possibility of a diplomatic solution under which Iran would follow the example of Libya in voluntarily giving up its nuclear program. Besides, once having played out the diplomatic string, and thereby having demonstrated that to him force is truly a last resort, Bush would be in a stronger political position to endorse John McCain's formula that the only thing worse than bombing Iran would be allowing Iran to build a nuclear bomb—and not just to endorse that assessment, but to act on it.

If this is what Bush intends to do, it goes, or should go, without saying that his overriding purpose is to ensure the security of this country in accordance with the vow he took upon becoming President, and in line with his pledge not to stand by while one of the world's most dangerous regimes threatens us with one of the world's most dangerous weapons.

But there is, it has been reported, another consideration that is driving Bush. According to a recent news story in the New York Times, for example, Bush has taken to heart what "[o]fficials from 21 governments in and around the Middle East warned at a meeting of Arab leaders in March, namely, "that Iran's drive for atomic technology could result in the beginning of 'a grave and destructive nuclear arms race in the region.'" Which is to say that he fears that local resistance to Iran's bid for hegemony in the greater Middle East through the acquisition of nuclear weapons could have even more dangerous consequences than a passive capitulation to that bid by the Arab countries. For resistance would spell the doom of all efforts to stop the spread of nuclear weapons, and it would vastly increase the chances of their use.

I have no doubt that this ominous prospect figures prominently in the president's calculations. But it seems evident to me that the survival of Israel, a country to which George W. Bush has been friendlier than any president before him, is also of major concern to him, a concern fully coincident with his worries over a Middle Eastern arms race.

Much of the world has greeted Ahmadinejad's promise to wipe Israel off the map with something close to insouciance. In fact, it could almost be said of the Europeans that they have been more upset by Ahmadinejad's denial that a Holocaust took place sixty years ago than by his determination to set off one of his own as soon as he acquires the means to do so. In a number of European countries, Holocaust denial is a crime, and the European Union only recently endorsed that position. Yet for all their retrospective remorse over the wholesale slaughter of Jews back then, the Europeans seem no readier to lift a finger to prevent a second Holocaust than they were the first time around.

Not so George W. Bush, a man who knows evil when he sees it and who has demonstrated an unfailingly courageous willingness to endure vilification and contumely in setting his face against it. It now remains to be seen whether this President, battered more mercilessly and with less justification than any other in living memory, and weakened politically by the enemies of his policy in the Middle East in general and Iraq in particular, will find it possible to take the only action that can stop Iran from following through on its evil intentions both toward us and toward Israel. As an American and as a Jew, I pray with all my heart that he will.

7

The Right of World Jewry to Criticize Israel

Moshe Halbertal

The subject of this book relates to the legitimacy, or the boundaries, of Diaspora Jewry's criticism of Israel and its actions. I must note that as I compose these words, it is an hour before we begin *Yom Hazikaron*, Israel's Memorial Day, when we mourn the fallen friends and families in the wars that we fought and are still fighting. And this reminds me that for every criticism that is done here, in the U.S., someone else—far away —pays the price for it. To say this is not, God forbid, a recommendation for silence. By no means is this a call for exiting the debate, or for paternalism or distance towards the issues involved. One cannot feel solidarity with another without it being legitimate to criticize the other.

I would, however, like to propose three limitations on such criticism.

First, be informed. Remember that you cannot raise a serious criticism of Israel based on an image you saw yesterday on CNN or in an article here or there, because in the war of images, Israel truly is on the losing side. That is because this conflict involves an asymmetry of threat. Israel's threat is invisible, it is not captured easily by image. But our actions to defend ourselves are quite easily captured by images, and some of those images are hard to watch. But images are by their nature taken out of context, freezing a single moment out of the whole situation.

What we need in criticism is what I would call a healthy iconoclasm. A very dear important rabbi once came to Israel around the time of the Oslo Agreements, and he had been very much against them. He challenged me on this issue—me as one who is religious, as well. Yet, even as he attacked my support of the agreements, he knew nothing of the situation. I asked him how many Palestinians live in the West Bank and

Gaza, and he could not come up with an answer. I asked him where is Nablus, where is this, where is that—he knew nothing. This is not to suggest that information will change a particular position. It is just to say that criticism directed from here in the U.S. to Israel should be informed, if it is to be serious, and taken seriously.

Second, in raising a critique, one should perform a certain exercise in empathy. To illustrate: suppose one thinks that Israel ought not to carry out any targeted killing (to take an issue that comes up repeatedly in the ethics of defense in an asymmetrical war against terror). If that is your position, then you must place yourself in the mind of a person living in Sderot, in the Negev, living with the constant bombing of Qassam rockets. If, after taking that step, you are still willing to make the same argument, then I tell you *yashar koach*, point well-made. But you must first position yourself there.

Similarly, if you think that we have to indiscriminately destroy every single village that a Qassam is launched from, imagine that your son will have to pull the trigger. And he'll have to come back home and look at himself in the mirror afterwards. If you think this way, you go through this empathetic thought process, and *then* you make the criticism – as I said, *Yashar Koach*, well-done.

And thirdly, in times of crisis, when there is a battle, for example, and a person is lying wounded, the last thing that is expected of me is to begin to argue with him as to whether he acted right in getting to that point. You don't challenge at that moment; you just extend your hand.

And this calls back the year 1938, the more general theme of this conference. In 1938, my father celebrated his bar mitzvah in a small shtetl called Landshut, in Galicia, and he was one of three million Jews in the larger region. At the time, the Polish-Jewish community was basically divided into three groups: a million or so Bundists, a million ultra-Orthodox Hasidim, and a million Zionists, roughly. My father belonged to an ultra-Orthodox Hasidic family, and grew up in a home that was ferociously anti-Zionist, as Zionism claimed to provide a secular alternative to Jewish identity, a rebellion against God's claim to history. My father himself survived the war, but his family was completely annihilated. In certain times of crisis, one does not ask, "How did you get here—who was right and who was wrong." You just extend a hand.

Are we in a time of crisis today? This is a very complicated thing to assess—when is the present moment in "the midst of crisis," or, alternatively, when is it time to voice criticism? One really has to think it through, in all its complexity. For example, we should avoid the easy language of a "clash of civilizations." I do not think this applies to the present conflict, which is in many ways still a local conflict between Israel and the Palestinians and between Israel and some of her neighbors. It is not a clash of civilizations. And in that respect it is not 1938. But we are in a deep debate, and Israel does not know which way to go, and this is, in fact, a kind of crisis. So one must be very careful in addressing criticism toward Israel at this moment, keeping in mind the limitations I propose here.

Again, these limitations are by no means a call for silence. But they do call for humility, at least some act of humbling. I remember when I was a soldier in the Lebanese war and a Hasidic rebbe criticized Israel for not taking over Beirut. I couldn't help wondering how many of his Hasidim were there. Humility, however, is not silence; quite the contrary. At this time we are seeking a partnership, a genuine partnership, with our counterparts in America. Israel, today especially, is in great need of American Jewish support, and the support of the U.S. in general. If you say to someone, "Be a partner, but you're not allowed to have a voice," the alternative to voice is exit. And we don't want exit. Nor do we want paternalism, or a view of "us" and "others."

In that respect, what I do fear with regard to criticism from the Diaspora today is a lack of solidarity. As an Israeli, I myself would stop feeling solidarity with Israel at the moment I stop having this vicarious embarrassment at what Israelis do. As in thinking, "it's not mine, it's the action of others." We don't want there to be the Israeli and the American Jewish, or the American, point of view.

My experience is that there is, after all, no unique American-Jewish point of view. Every argument we have back home, we have here in America as well. I remember I had the opportunity to be part of the group drafting the ethics code of the army, and I tended to receive two complaints – both of which I get here, as well. One came from the right, basically: "Why the hell do you sacrifice our soldiers to defend civilian life on the other side? Just bomb them." The other one was from the left, demanding that if we were involved, necessarily, in harming innocent people, *don't shoot*. Stop participating. Usually this is the argument you here in both places, in some form, in the U.S. and in Israel. And it is very hard, in contrast, to make a reasonable, sensible argument that takes into account the complexity of the situation.

So I must say, there isn't an American Jewish point of view, as opposed to an Israeli point of view. We are now in a deep debate about what we ought to do, what is the way forward for Israel. And as partners, we share in this same debate on both sides of the ocean.

8

The Ethical Limits and Ways
of Criticizing Israel

Blu Greenberg

In November 2001, I was flying back to New York with a friend I had come to know through dialogue. She was a sophisticated soft-spoken woman of Egyptian origin, part of an intellectual elite, who held a position of power in an international body that was affiliated with the United Nations. We were coming back from a dialogue meeting and discussing some aspects of the sessions. At one point on the plane, she said to me that Israel started the four wars of its history. We spent the next half hour on that, mostly with me refuting her claims, citing the facts about the 1947 Partition plan, the response of the Arab states, the provocation that led to the War of Independence, the Egyptian vote to nationalize the Suez in 1956, the threat to annihilate Israel in 1967, the surprise attack of Yom Kippur. Afterwards she said to me that this wasn't her view, but that of the "Arab street." Rather than beat a dead horse, I resisted the temptation to say, "Well it's your job to try to clean up your streets." We simply went on to other subjects. But as we were about to land in New York, she interrupted with what was obviously on her mind. "I must take back what I said a half hour ago," she said. "Israel *did* start the four wars —by being there."

That was six years ago. Today it's much worse. The situation is more complex and more difficult. Dialogue has moved, I'm sorry to say, from a two-state solution to a single-state. There is no real outcry against Iranian President Ahmadinejad in the world press. It is in this context that we must examine the question of ethical limits of criticism of Israel in matters of national security. In these vulnerable times Israel is engaged not only in a physical battle for survival, but in a war of narratives, in which the other side is winning, with a shocking degree of demonization of Israel. It is totally reversing the image of Israel and the reality of Israel, undoing the former image of the Jewish State as a tiny nation, David facing Goliath. In this context, every criticism about Israel's exercise of power—its army, the Mossad, the wall, the occupation, the refugee camps, the checkpoints, the closures, the destruction of homes of families of suicide bombers—criticism of all of these defense mechanisms, or acts of deterrence, contributes to the image of Israel as a rogue state. And it is an image that is regrettably widely seen in the world.

However, I am not one of those who think that we ought to stifle criticism. Short of giving away state secrets, the only ethical limit that I would apply to criticism by Diaspora Jews would be that of the truth. And my dispute with some Diaspora critics is that, by and large, they speak half-truths that contribute to Israel's vulnerability. In a certain sense half-truths are as dangerous as outright lies.

Some examples of half-truths: The wall. In some places you could barely see the wall but in some places it is awful. It is ugly, it mars the landscape, but worse than that it separates families and friends. If I were a Palestinian I'd feel violated by a wall built in my city. That is the truth. And I should be able to speak that truth and express sympathy for families who have a wall blocking their lives. But it is only a half-truth. The wall was built not for spite but for self-protection. It is not apartheid but rather a fixed object that has reduced terror attacks by 65 percent, saving "x" number of Israeli lives. At the very least, Diaspora critics of the wall must acknowledge those facts. If it is too difficult for them to say, "yes the wall, but…" let them say it in reverse: The wall was built for protection against terror, but it is ugly, cruel, unnecessary, over the top, etc. Or whatever else represents their decent and admirable desires for the dignity of Palestinians.

Another example: the occupation. Many of my friends on the political left are vocal in their criticism of occupation: it should never have been there in the first place, we should get out of there today, and so on. Occupation does represent a loss of autonomy, freedom, power, people with no homeland, things that we know could really be great losses. But the whole truth is that even after conquering these lands, defending itself in a war of aggression in which the Arab states threatened to make the Mediterranean flow in a sea of blood, Israel stretched out its hand in peace, not once but many times. But it found no takers, no recognition, only a stubborn enemy unwilling to compromise. To vilify the occupation and to express feelings of sympathy would in fact be noble if it were the whole truth about Israel as occupier. But as a flawed half-truth it fails everyone. It feeds the fantasy of negative revenge by those who are occupied, and it ignores the Israelis who suffer.

I can go up and down the line with half truths. Checkpoints, for example. These are caricatured in the Arab press—and in the Western press—as dehumanizing. In fact they are not as barbaric as depicted, and body searches are very rare. They are oppressive, with the long lines and delays, and I know that Israeli soldiers would rather take any assignment other than checkpoints, because there is so much hatred there. But the whole truth is that they are used for Israel's protection, and that even with checkpoints some terrorists get through. And there is no additional protection against suicide bombers in most Palestinian cities, but only rejoicing and martyrdom for the bomber, celebration in his community, and reward for his family. And I've never heard a Diaspora critic wonder why Arabs do not need to have their pocket books or briefs-cases examined as they enter an Arab movie theater or restaurant or wedding hall. The critics are right to say that Israeli soldiers made a bad judgment in delaying an ambulance that carried a pregnant woman. But the critics must add that similar ambulances were found to have grenades and bullets hidden in their floor boards. And the critic must add that hundreds of Arab women give birth every day in Israel, in Israeli hospitals, and are treated exactly as Jewish women are, and that Israeli hospitals are blind when it comes to race and color. And that an Arab father of seven from the city of Shu'afat received a liver transplant at Hadassah Hospital, transplanted from the body of a Jew, even though the middle son of this Arab father was linked to Hamas.

And going back further, to 1948, to the refugee camps—those "bleeding sores," those "breeding grounds for terror." I visited two such camps and I could not help but think of the nice homes in Baka and in Katamon and in Kfar Saba that the parents and grandparents of the residents came from, which they still considered to be their homes—and to which they longed to go back. But the whole truth is that unlike the unfortunate refugees from other countries, Palestinian refugees—whether because their leaders urged them to flee or because they heard nearby battles and fled out of fright—these refugees were never welcomed by their brothers and sisters. They were never integrated into the rest of the Palestinian population, never accepted or allowed to accept the countless offers by Israel and the world community to resettle them in decent homes that would give them a head start on a new life, something that all refugees are entitled to.

Many critics on the left have bought into the story of the "Massacre of Jenin," as it is called. An on-site exhibit and a movie have been created, along with a book and hundreds of op-eds in the Arab world—all continuing to excoriate Israel over Jenin. But the larger truth is that Jenin was a breeding ground for wannabe suicide bombers, a base from which marauders and attackers set out for all the Israeli towns around Afula. And the targeted killings there, which cost Israel many losses, were an ethical choice on Israel's part not to increase the number of victims on the Arab side. Thus targeted killings was a moral choice, taken by Israel rather than bomb the homes of suicide bombers' families (I'm not sure it was such a great military choice, but that is another question).

So I am not saying we should close off the criticism; we should welcome it, in fact, but we should force it to stand up to the standard of whole-truth telling. Criticism of Israel must always be contextual, as should all criticism. And we have to be open to the possibility that criticism in certain areas is valid. I must point out that while I won't tolerate or idly stand by half truths, I have learned a lot from the critics on the left: there are moral gaps and lapses in judgment in the steps taken by Israel, together with missed opportunities and policies far more complex than I had thought. And still, with all that I can say that Israel has the most moral army in the world, is a model of the ethical use of power, a bastion of the democratic principles that I hold dear, a pursuer of peace and justice (even though unfortunately others have co-opted those terms).

I am not so naïve as to think that by my saying so—or anyone else likewise urging that criticism meet the standards of the whole truth and such—that critics of Israel, or even lovers of Israel, will comply. Critics are just not made that way. But to make the picture whole, we —as those who disagree with the half-truths—are obligated to fill out the facts and details, and not to let half-truths go by, out of weariness or hopelessness. It is our moral imperative to respond unrelentingly, respectfully, to half truths. We are not being asked to send our children to Gaza. We are not waiting by the radio every morning, in anxiety, to hear about skirmishes and losses in a war. But we can join Israel in the war of narratives.

And in a certain sense, criticism by Diaspora Jews gets much more attention in the press than that of others. We, too, have to invite ourselves into the public debate, to respond, and to make ourselves better informed, using the available resources. And for reality-testing we should not only use our own resources, but we should investigate some of the Arab websites, even the milder ones, and see what is out there. There is no antidote to criticism more potent than knowledge of the facts. We should arm our children with such knowledge. We should know enough to respond at dinner parties, instead of holding our tongues and complaining afterwards. We should be writing letters to the press and calling the media when we read or hear something expressed in a half-truths.

There is no need to deny valid criticism, and one can acknowledge the difficulties and imbalances at play here. But in responding to it, a first step is to become informed. The second is to take initiative. Not to sit reacting, but to go forward, in dialogue groups and discussion groups, and get our own organizations to make us better informed and to engage with others in dialogue. And that would take us to the third step: entering into dialogue with other Americans. With Protestants on divestment, with Catholics on Israel's protection of holy places, with Muslims on every issue that we face together. I am not suggesting that anyone give up their day job. But all this takes time and energy and initiative. We cannot wait for someone else to do it. We do not have to wait for a form letter to be sent to us. There is power in every one of us as individuals and we should act upon it.

In the final analysis Israel has chosen the ethical use of power. There are always compromises and challenges and pitfalls, always a margin of error. Israel has made the most valiant and incredible effort to reduce error, to act with restraint in the face of great provocation, to remain moral in a set of choices that are at best very difficult. We must keep up with Israel, and with its loving critics, to make sure that along with the criticism, along with the compassion, along with the desire for justice for all, the larger and noble story of Israel will be told.

9

Diaspora Criticism and Advocacy

Jeff Helmreich

About ten years ago, we celebrated the end of Jewish political identity. More than that, it was the end of Jewish group identity entirely. The leading social scientists of the Diaspora, even those commissioned by Jewish organizations, all reported back that those organizations had become much less relevant. American Jews were turning inward, focusing less on tribal concerns like survival and continuity, and more on themselves: Who am I? How do I express my Jewishness? What's the best outlet for my spirituality and my prayer, or my family's prayer? A Diaspora once stirred by "Let my People Go," inspired by *"Tikkun Olam"* and emboldened by *"Am Yisrael Chai,"* now turned to private Kabbalah meditations. We stopped being "The Jewish People" and became, simply, Jews. Artists. Accountants. Parents.

Then, as if on cue, history conspired to change all that. Israel suddenly vaulted back to the stage of world events, as the hopeful Camp David summit burst into the apocalyptic Al-Aqsa Intifada, igniting a war that still rages with no end in sight. The United States was attacked in the most brutal and humbling way, sparking a much larger war that unleashed its own apocalyptic clashes. It is, of course, easy to distinguish between the new threats and those of 1938—any two time periods have trivial differences. But it is far more instructive to note the similarities: once again, the gravest threats to world peace come not from self-interested, or strategically motivated, forces but from genocidal ones (and the world's powers tolerate it).

How did all this affect the individual American Jew? One clue could be found on American campuses over the past decade. That's where it is

67

most clear that a new Jewish movement has sprung up, though it reaches far beyond the academy. The movement is collective, survivalist, and single-minded in its purpose: defend Israel. Sometimes the campaign is called "*Hasbarah*"—generously translated as "explanation," as in explaining Israel's side of the story. The force is reactive, fending off an unrelenting assault.

This movement has come to dominate Jewish identity and drive on American campuses today—at least among those who choose to identify Jewishly. Where once Jews went to college to become doctors, today they go to be spin doctors. Once the rousing cry of young Jewish activists was "Let my people go!"; today it's "Resolution 242 does not call for a complete withdrawal."

I want to evaluate this movement and how it relates to the issue of Diaspora criticism of Israel. The movement is, after all, something to take seriously. It has been remarkable in its sweep, its energy, and—above all—its failure. Indeed, even as more Jewish organizational funds and projects have poured into the *Hasbarah* campaign, support for Israel has become even less politically correct, less academically or journalistically fashionable. It is unclear whether this would have happened anyway, or even become worse without the Jewish counterattack.

What is clear is that the new movement comes from somewhere other than the detached vantage point where we question the ethics and honesty of criticizing Israel. That is not because the new movement is ethically challenged; it isn't. But it is facing an enemy that it perceives as advancing even as we speak, and fighting back is so urgent, and such a monumental undertaking, that it crowds out all other concerns.

In a strange way, Jewish students come to this debate with what Henry Louis Gates, Jr., calls a counter-narrative—a private, esoteric version of events that a minority group clings to when the accepted history is against them. They come with an understanding of the Middle East from deep in their blood, their gut, their *kischkes*, honed in households and Hebrew schools securely insulated from the presuppositions that support the dominant narrative on campuses and in journalism schools. But it isn't long before they hear that dominant narrative: that Israel is an occupying colonizer, standing in the way of Palestinian independence. That Palestinian so-called "terrorism" is in fact justified, if at times overreactive, resistance to an oppressive policy that Israel started, and refuses to stop. That Jewish statehood is racist, at least where it extends to the West Bank and the wall. That the Middle East conflict is caused mostly by Israeli policy; that American support for Israel is imbalanced and unfair—and hurting America.

The problem for Jewish students is that these tenets—so at odds with what they thought they knew—are in fact the default, conventional wisdom at universities. So there is a radical disconnect between the accepted story and the history these Jewish students have already learned: that Israel, basically, has always meant well towards its neighbors, has strove for nothing more than to be a democracy and a safe haven for Jews, but not at the expense of any non-Jews. And above all, they learned that Israel's most controversial steps—checkpoints, closures, indeed its very presence in Palestinian towns in the West Bank—were reluctantly carried out as last resorts, for its own survival, all the while desperate for a partner that would make them unnecessary.

This version of events, of course, is not just different but nearly the opposite of the dominant view, and that leads to alienation. The Jewish students feel that that they don't speak the same language or see the same world as their surrounding culture. They grow to mistrust the academic orthodoxy that, they feel, has betrayed them and is incapable of accepting them—and they shun the basic principles and ideas, and even the terms, that their liberal classmates take as starting points.

But Jews are not African-Americans, the group that Gates had in mind with respect to counter-narratives. They differ especially in one crucial respect: Jews are otherwise at home in the university and the larger power structure, and in its discourse and rules. They've had power and access to it, and feel they can navigate the dominant reality and even change it. They can persuade others, not only in classrooms but in courtrooms, congressional committees and op-ed pages. They can make a difference.

These two distinct feelings—of pariah and power—mix uneasily in the Jewish student's mind as he first enters the campus arena, or in the Jewish activist who first debates a Palestinian. He thinks everyone in the room is wrong, dangerously and unfairly so, but also that he can—and therefore must—do something about it. A *Hasbarah* advocate is born.

There is something unnatural, maybe not altogether healthy, about this new path that so many young Jews find themselves forced to take. In a more familiar path, adolescence gives way to an internal struggle, as cherished values and ideas are challenged and re-examined. Whatever the final result – a transformation or a fortified return – the process itself is a valuable part of growing up, of maturing, and of making our ideas truly our own.

For the new generation of Israel activists, however, this process is stunted: they're at war with others before they've had any time to interrogate themselves. They're defending ideas they haven't had time to develop and think through.

The irony is that this premature devotion to the fight is part of the reason that the Israel advocates are losing it so colossally. They have not stepped out of their roles as debaters long enough to take seriously the questions they need to answer, or to learn the language in which to answer them. Instead, their confidence in Israel's rightness is so deep and unshakable that they react in shock. Challenges are not merely "misguided"; they are seen as "ridiculous," or at best very ignorant.

But from the perspective of an educated outsider, it is not ridiculous to consider Israel the culprit in its conflict. If you value absolute equality, it is far from ludicrous to see Israel's explicit "Jewishness"—especially if one does not know the extent of its legal or political impact, or lack thereof—as favoritist. If you value the struggle of colonized people against imperialism, it is not hard to blurrily link Israeli soldiers with the lighter-skinned, Western-allied conquerors of familiar colonial regimes —after all, the Israelis are the ones in uniforms and tanks, the Palestinians in the native-looking garb. And it is even easier to do so when the alleged "colonizers" have enemies who resemble Che Guevara, with their rhetoric of liberation and freedom and their positioning as underdogs. Most important, when you believe that all people—unconditionally –have the right to vote on the laws and policies imposed on them, it is not ridiculous to question Israel's impositions on West Bank Palestinians who don't vote in Israel's parliament, particularly when some of those impositions—like the wall—can be harsh. And given all this, it becomes less than ridiculous to think that terrorism is just an overreaction to policies that even Americans would fight to avoid.

It takes a sophisticated, nuanced insider's grasp of the conflict to know why these concerns are ill-informed. It is far from obvious that today's Israeli role in the West Bank—which looks exactly like yesterday's occupation—is in fact an entirely new development: that Israel's military presence there is reluctant and meant to end soon, and that, like the wall, it is largely a temporary response to violence rather than a long-standing cause of it. Moreover, it is extremely counter-intuitive to see that the violence directed at Israel is largely aimed against Palestinian independence, rather than in favor of it.

All this is not too complex to explain. But it is not the superficial, obvious interpretation, especially if the interpreter is a liberal, rights-oriented university student who studies this conflict along with many others. And Israel advocates are ill-equipped to reach such an interpreter, because they never seriously entertained the rights-based, or equality-based, challenges that motivate him or her. Today's young lobbyists do not, themselves, lose sleep over whether Israel is oppressing the Palestinians. And for that reason they are uniquely unqualified to defend against charges that it is doing so. When they try, citing a tired litany of terrorist atrocities and textbook incitements, they come across like law-and-order cops talking to visionary poets in the 1960s: a culture clash so strong that persuasion is impossible.

Worse, still, are the few attempts that do address Israel's critics "on their terms." Egged on by polls taken in Washington about six years ago, a handful of Israeli advocates and even Israeli officials have begun dressing up their anti-terror routine in the language of rights, equality and freedom —like shouting the names of favorite teams to a throng of sports fans. But these spokespeople come across plainly like manipulators, because they use the new talk to reach the same old punch line: we're good, they're bad. Only instead of "they're bad" meaning savage terrorists, it now means "human rights abusers." The problem is that "we're good, they're bad"—no matter how it is formulated—is just not the soul-searching, hopeful, visionary, kind of message that would move a pure-minded activist. It is spin, and that's what it sounds like. It is why even the best Israeli "television stars" come across as "persuasive," or slick, while the Palestinian stars come across as heartfelt and anguished.

In short, unflinching advocacy for Israel is ineffective, even *as* advocacy. But it is also ethically problematic. Just think how we, as American Jews, would feel about another group—say African Americans or Irish Americans or particularly Arab Americans—that never spoke out against its own transgressors, here or abroad. We'd think of blind support as exactly what it sounds like: blind. Often morally blind. If so, then we dare not be that way ourselves, especially when we can afford not to be: Israel, after all, is not the culprit in the conflict, but is largely reacting to a war launched by forces that prefer a bloody conflict to a two-state solution. If we are so sure that Israel wants peace and regrets any civilian death, then we should recoil in horror at the few instances where it errs and causes such death (even by accident). For example, we might criticize the leveling of an entire building to take out a single terrorist like Sheikh

Shehadeh in 2003, or similar occurrences during the Lebanon invasion. We praise Israel for having the kind of agonizing pangs of conscience that force it to reconsider so many aerial bombings, and instead risk its own soldiers going house to house. But that praise is disingenuous unless we suffer the same pangs here—and voice them.

Of course some such pangs are misplaced. Certain Diaspora critics of Israel continue to define themselves as peaceniks fighting against zealots for Zion, or as two-state advocates against Greater Israel. In echoing this outdated dispute, they misleadingly, slanderously, drape today's reluctant Israeli policy in the flag of land grabbing conquistadores. This is a libelous blow to the Israeli soldier who hates checkpoint duty and the Israeli government that would rather call him off, and to the majority of Israelis who are desperate to convince the world that they, too, want a two-state solution and have all but banished "Greater Israel" from their political landscape. But these American critics remain too attached to their own self-image, as opponents of "Greater Israel," to allow Israelis the benefit of their own hard-won, soul-searching abandonment of expansionist ideology.

For their part, the rightist spin doctors, too, fail to stand up for their cause. They are not only unconvincingly supportive of Israel but also, paradoxically, insufficiently warm in their support. That is because the new generation of Israel advocates do not trust their audience with their true feelings, or with feelings altogether. Instead, they vigorously redecorate pro-Israel arguments in universalistic guise, as though—by an almost magical coincidence—their concern is not Israel, per se, but world peace, the "war on terror," the furtherance of economic prosperity, the "clash of civilizations," or the integrity of international law.

In hiding their particularistic side, Diaspora activists have not only made their spin hollow, dry and unattractive. They have also betrayed their soul, given up that gut-level force that Shlomo Carlebach drew out with his protest song, *Am Yisrael Chai*, "the people of Israel live." It was that simple anthem that helped inspire the Soviet Jewry movement. And what can be more particularistic, more un-spun, than "Let my people go"? It is not "let *the* people go," or "enforce these universal rights." It is about *my* people, and it is spoken in the raw, primitive mode of a command. Every downtrodden people, including the Palestinians, reserve a place in their lexicon for this mode.

The journalist Daniel Pearl arguably made his living putting things in universal terms, translating events for American readers and sensibilities.

But he became immortal because of one moment, his final moment, when he said his last words, pointedly facing his executioners: "I am a Jew. My father is Jewish." That, perhaps, captures the most appropriate model of a Diaspora critic: that of family. A close relative is rebuked when she does something wrong, defended heatedly when she is defamed, and through it all warmly—and particularistically—loved.

10

Saving American Jewry: Demography, Politics, and Destiny

Jack Wertheimer

When Benjamin Netanyahu spoke at the General Assembly of the United Jewish Communities in November 2006, he memorably invoked parallels between current complacency about the looming Iranian nuclear threat and the passivity of the world community during the late 1930s in the face of the mounting menace posed by Nazi Germany. Despite the worrisome nature of the current challenge, I have my doubts as to the aptness of the parallel. I certainly would not argue that for American Jewry it is 1938 all over again. For better and worse, we face very different challenges in this country than we did seventy years ago, although, as I will suggest at the end of this essay, we are beset by a paralysis quite similar to that suffered by our forbearers, albeit one that concerns very different issues.

I

The comparison to 1938 is actually a helpful way to examine the current condition of American Jewry. I begin with some of the most obvious differences:

- In 1938, the United States was only gradually coming out of the Great Depression. Jews, like their Gentile compatriots, were living in hard times. Only in the post-war era would they come to experience the great economic boom that would transform the Jewish community into a largely upper middle class population. Today by contrast, American Jews have benefited from decades of economic expansion, which has enabled Jews to become the most economically successful ethnic group

in the country. The numbers of Jews on the lists of wealthiest Americans are vastly out of proportion to the Jewish percentage of the general
population. Twenty years ago, Charles Silberman vividly captured this
success story in his book, *A Certain People*, writing of the rise of the
"two Shapiro's," the Shapiro who headed the Dupont corporation and
the Shapiro who was president at the time of Princeton University.
Corporate America and the prestige universities discriminated against
Jews in 1938; today we take it for granted that Jews hold the highest
offices and sit on the boards of both kinds of institutions. We also take
it for granted that the third wealthiest American is a Jew, one who has
just committed to giving tens of millions of dollars to Jewish causes on
an annual basis. And we think nothing of the fact that major high-tech
companies, such as Dell and Oracle, were founded by Jews, as was
Google, whose young co-founders are Jews. In short, Jews not only
earn well but no longer worry about quotas and employment barriers,
as they did in 1938.

- Unlike in 1938, Jews are no longer victims of housing discrimination
  or other forms of social exclusion. These, along with employment
  discrimination, were the major forms of anti-Semitism seventy years
  ago. When my parents looked to rent an apartment in the borough
  of Queens in the early 1940s, they encountered signs on apartment
  buildings announcing: "No Jews, Negroes and Dogs Allowed." Such
  blatant discrimination no longer exists today—and if it does, tell Abe
  Foxman who will get it to stop.

- Which brings me to another important shift: Jews were far more timid
  in asserting their rights in 1938. While defense agencies existed since
  the first two decades of the twentieth century, only in the 1930s and
  1940s did they embark on a battle against exclusionary anti-Semitism
  and discrimination more generally. The year 1938 and the first years
  of World War II were not the "good old days." Those years marked a
  period when anti-Semitism reached its historical zenith in this country—as it did everywhere in the world. Jews and their organizations
  were cautious then. They felt besieged and watched their every step.
  And individual Jews also were careful about where they would walk
  in the city. Jewish kids could expect to encounter anti-Semitic baiters
  in school, and to suffer a thrashing if they blundered onto the wrong
  street. For the most part, young Jews today are spared such insults.
  They are shocked, simply shocked, if they ever encounter anti-Semitic
  thuggery. And their parents will do anything to spare their children any
  exposure to anti-Semitism, which perhaps is one of the reasons they
  take their Jewishness so much for granted. They never have to think
  about what makes them different and how they feel about a Jewish
  identity that marks them as distinctive.

- In 1938, Jewish organizational life was impoverished. Just as there
  was a religious depression in church life, so too there was a decline
  in synagogue membership. Rates of participation in religious services

were low, as was the contribution Jews made to Jewish organizations. Although today, many Jewish organizations, let alone Jewish foundations, operate in high style, with the fanciest of technology and well-appointed offices, seventy years ago Jewish life was conducted in modest, if not shabby, facilities.

- As for the image of Judaism: in 1938 few Americans paid it much heed or had any idea of what Judaism might be about. When Louis Finkelstein, then the president of the Jewish Theological Seminary, embarked on a program in the late 1940s to broadcast Judaism to America via the vehicles of radio and television, the Jewish Museum and interfaith conversations, he was a pioneer. Today, we take it for granted that Jews and Judaism are featured prominently in the media. When former president Clinton apologized to the American public for his dalliance with a young Jewish woman, he quoted from the Jewish High Holiday liturgy. Every president of the United States in recent decades has held a Hanukkah candle-lighting ceremony at the White House. It is unthinkable to convene conferences on religion in America without including Jewish representatives. None of this was evident in 1938 when the mainline Protestant churches held sway.

I can go on with other examples of just how much the lives of Jews today are so different and so much better than in 1938. Simply put, for Jews as individuals, life in this country has evolved over the past seventy years in very positive ways. Jews have come to expect virtually unlimited access: no field of endeavor bars them. And in a few prominent fields, such as the media, politics, the academy, the legal profession, and Wall Street, Jews are over-represented relative to their proportion of the populace. In recent decades, Jewish women have participated actively in the labor force and, like their male counterparts, have risen to high offices in many fields. And our young people are numerically over-represented at the very universities and colleges that still in 1938, and afterwards, imposed quotas on Jewish enrollment. As individuals, then, the story-line since 1938 has been about the opening of the American mind, economy, government and society to Jews.

II

The story for Jews as a collective is, of course, far more complex. But certainly, we should note some of the major assets the Jewish collective has acquired since 1938.

1. Most important: we have a Jewish state in Israel. For affiliated Jews, Israel is a living part of their lives. Approximately one third of American Jews have visited Israel, many on more than one occasion. Study in Israel

became far more common since 1967, as is the celebration of rites of passage. We still lack a good analysis of what Israel has meant to the Jewish lives of American Jews, but anyone who travels to Israel and witnesses the youth groups and adult missions can see that something quite profound and enjoyable is experienced by these visitors.

As American Jews struggle with some of their own internal problems, they have come to regard Israel as a fertile environment to educate their youth about Jewish peoplehood, religion, and civilization. Birthright Israel is a remarkable experiment predicated on the assumption that young American Jews can have a transformational experience that will stimulate them to live and identify as Jews for years to come. In the summer of 2007, nearly 25,000 Jews between the ages of eighteen and twenty-six are scheduled to leave for the ten-day Birthright trips. It's really an extraordinary program, without parallel. Which other people sends its youth abroad for a free trip in such massive numbers?

Israel is a remarkable asset of the Jewish people. But let us note the role reversal that has taken place since 1938: Before the creation of the state and into its first two decades, Israel was a philanthropic cause of American Jews. Today it is at least as much a lifeline for an American Jewish community that needs Israel to provide Jewish sustenance and inspiration, especially for its youth.

2. A second asset is the revitalized Orthodox community. In 1938, Orthodoxy was in decline. Surveys taken in the middle decades of the twentieth century demonstrated a high rate of defection from Orthodoxy. Some contemporary observers doubted Orthodoxy would survive long after the passing of the immigrant generation. Today, its population is growing due to its high birth rate. But equally important, Orthodox Jews no longer feel on the defensive. In contrast to their liberalizing co-religionists, they are retaining the allegiance of their youth. They are also benefiting from the altered religious environment, in which traditional religion has become more assertive as it has become clear that liberal religion does not satisfy. Since the 1960s the pews of liberal churches have been emptying, even as conservative churches have experienced dramatic growth. The pews of Orthodox synagogues tend also to be filled, even as those of most non-Orthodox ones stand relatively empty for much of the year.

Moreover, Orthodoxy is gaining greater sway in Jewish public life because it is able to provide leaders. Where once there were so-called secular Jewish organizations—federations, community relations groups, social welfare institutions, and the like—that were not particularly receptive to Orthodox personnel, today these same agencies employ significant numbers of Orthodox Jews. And then there is the outreach industry: non-Orthodox groups cannot field a sufficient number of rabbis to care for the needs of their own members, let alone hold communal positions, whereas Orthodoxy produces a surfeit of rabbis. Chabad is spreading like wildfire across the country, opening on campuses that have a scant Reform and Conservative presence, creating Hebrew schools that compete directly with established schools, and serving as personal religious trainers to Jews. Everyone knows there is a long line of shluchim, emissaries, numbering in the hundreds, ready to be deployed as soon as a new site for a Chabad outpost is identified. Meanwhile, the Conservative and Reform and Reconstructionist and non-denominational seminaries keep multiplying, but between them they ordain not much more than 100 rabbis a year. In fact, Chabad business is so good that its Haredi competitors are angling for a piece of the action, developing programs of their own to train outreach rabbis.

For the first time in 200 years, Orthodoxy is ascendant—not only in this country but around the world. I note this not to overlook the significant challenges Orthodoxy faces—its internal rivalries, its disproportionately large population of poor Jews, its social problems—but the overall picture is one of vitality and growth, something that cannot be said of most other Jewish movements today.

3. The transformed field of Jewish education is still another asset. To its great credit, the American Jewish community has produced a rich panoply of schools and informal educational vehicles to educate its very youngest in their pre-school years, their oldest in all kinds of adult education classes, and those in between—children and teens and college students. Hundreds of day schools dot the land, easily 1800 supplementary schools educate our youth; teen programs, youth programs and trips to Israel are available to the post-Bar and Bat Mitzvah set. What makes this all the more remarkable is the haphazard way in which these efforts have sprung up in one community after the next. In an age of consumerism, Jewish parents enjoy a range of options from which to choose. If they want to provide a Jewish education to their children, they have an embarrassment of riches in the choices at their disposal.

The field of Jewish education was far more circumscribed seventy years ago. It relied heavily upon immigrant educators who more often than not taught in ramshackle surroundings. Today, teachers are home grown—although there are not nearly enough of them—and they rely upon new technologies to deliver an education. Internet and computer-driven programs augment Jewish learning—whether it is daf yomi online or classes taught by Israelis via internet hookup, whether its is Google searches to ferret out information or visually arresting materials now easily accessible in electronic form. All these are major advances. And then on the college level, we have experienced the explosion of Jewish studies, so that those young people who are interested can continue learning about things Jewish on college campuses. These are all important resources.

4. Many of these developments have been made possible by the expansion of Jewish philanthropy. Jewish studies programs have spread because Jewish donors have funded them. Day schools have mushroomed because enough funders have taken the lead in getting them off the ground. Birthright and other Israel study programs have become available because enough Jews have seen fit to invest in Jewish education. Fortunately, big donors are now spurring further advances in Jewish education by funding new curricula, attending to the needs of Jewish educators, creating umbrella agencies for every category of Jewish education—separate agencies for day schools, for supplementary schools, for early childhood programs, for youth activities, for summer camping.

These are all symptoms of the revitalization of Jewish life in this country and hold the promise of renewal.

III

There is however a big "but" to this litany of positives. For all of its strengths, the American Jewish community faces a set of intractable internal challenges that were barely on the horizon in 1938. Whereas in the first half of the twentieth century, the Jewish population surged, with wave upon wave of immigration, that is far less the case in our own time. Whereas in 1938 the great political need of the Jews was to win acceptance, today Jews are so well integrated that many see no difference between themselves and others. While at mid-century, American Jews were poised to engage in several decades of organizational activities, today we are in a state of demographic decline. In recent years, some demographers have challenged the estimated Jewish population figures put forth by the National Jewish Population Study of 2000-2001, claiming the figure of 5.2-5.5 million is too low. Instead, they project a population of six million or even slightly higher. None of these demographers is arguing that the Jewish community is growing. They are saying that previous estimates were too low. Even if the figure of six million is more accurate, the American Jewish population has not kept pace despite the influx of a million Jewish immigrants over the past sixty years.

Put simply, we are losing more Jews to death than we are gaining through birth. And this trend is likely to get worse as the population ages and younger Jews fail to marry when it is still possible to conceive children or, when they do marry, they have small families. The great social revolution of our time is the long delay in marriage. A young scholar of my acquaintance refers to the twenties and thirties as a "black hole" in Jewish life. Young Jews who don't marry tend to remain disconnected from Jewish institutions for fifteen, twenty, or twenty-five years after their Bar or Bat Mitzvah, which may make it harder to bring them back once they do marry. Without the responsibility of a family, they tend to live at a remove from organized Jewish life, connecting only episodically. As the sociologist Steven M. Cohen has observed, the key divides in Jewish life today are between Jews married to Jews, the unmarried and the intermarried. The former tend to engage with Jewish education, religious institutions, and the Jewish people. The unmarried tend to be at a remove. They regard Jewish institutions as focused primarily on families. And as they have internalized the message that all holidays and religious observances are only for the sake of children, they rightly wonder whether there is a point to affiliation if they have no children.

And then there is the other great divide: between Jews married to Jews and those married to non-Jews. The latter are far less likely than the former to join a synagogue, give to Jewish causes, live in areas of relatively dense Jewish concentration, befriend other Jews—and raise their children as Jews. In only two communities, data suggest a rising percentage of intermarried Jews claiming to raise their children as Jews. In the bulk of communities studied, roughly 30 percent claim they are raising their children as Jews. Presumably, if 70 percent of children from intermarried homes are not being raised as Jews, they will not identify as Jewish.

In the spring of 2007, I conducted a correspondence with a young man who claims to reflect the views of young adults raised in intermarried homes. His self-characterization is eye-opening. He writes that he and his friends refer to themselves as "FrankenJews" and openly joke about their "mongrel" identity. These are his words, not mine. And what do they want? They regard efforts to create barriers to intermarriage as a throwback to the middle ages; instead, they seek a Judaism that will make room for their non-Jewish "patrimony:" they imagine a Judaism that will enable them to fuse the Jewish and non-Jewish components of their fractured identity. Hundreds of thousands of such young people now exist somewhere in the orbit of the Jewish community, usually at a remove, but in some cases closer to the center. They will increasingly demand of the Jewish community that it create a religiously syncretistic space for their dual-religion identities.

Taken together, low birth-rates and high intermarriage rates are sapping the demographic vitality of the Jewish community—the Orthodox population excepted. A recent compilation of data on national surveys conducted by the most authoritative polling agency (the National Opinion Research Center at the University of Chicago, or NORC) marshals considerable evidence for the relatively advanced age of the American Jewish population. Among religious groups, only liberal Protestants exceed Jews in this regard; among ethnic groups, only Americans of British ancestry do. Among Americans of all kinds, moreover, Jews have the fewest number of siblings, the smallest household size, and the second lowest number of children under eighteen at home.

As the majority of children raised in intermarried homes are not even educated as Jews, we can expect a very significant fall off in the American Jewish population over the coming decades. And as high percentages of Jews intermarry, the likelihood of a Jewish population shrinkage is great. Some argue that this is unimportant: quality, not quantity, counts. I doubt that politicians looking for votes would agree. Some argue that the vitality of the community depends mainly on its engagement; true enough, but who will populate those communities? As the boomer generation and its elders age, there will be a significant fall off in the size of the American Jewish population. And the gap between engaged Jews and the vast army of Jews raised in intermarried homes, living a syncretistic form of religious life, will widen.

The second worrisome trend affecting the group life of Jews is the decline in affiliation and connection to the Jewish people, as ever more Jews devote ever more of their energies either to highly individualistic activities, divorced from any collective Jewish endeavor, or to universalistic causes.

The contrast to the mid-twentieth century is dramatic. "What distinguishes the Jew from the non-Jew is, increasingly, not a specific ethic, religious discipline, or language, but the intensity and pervasiveness of his organizational commitments and activities…. At present Jewish culture in the United States is predominantly what Jews do under the auspices of Jewish organizations." So wrote Harold Weisberg, dean of the Graduate School of Brandeis University, in 1964, astutely identifying the popular, if not predominant, form Jewish engagement took in the post-war era. Other contemporary observers also noted the extent to which theirs was a time of joining. American Jews in record numbers became members of synagogues, Jewish Community Centers, local agencies and national organizations; they contributed to federation campaigns; and in other ways enacted their Jewishness through association. Referring to these patterns, a major sociological study of the time took note of the "overwhelming" variety of Jewish organizations on the local level, "the critical role they played to help mediate the crisis in Jewish identity" and their contribution to "Jewish group survival." A half century later, the climate has changed considerably, and all of Jewish organizational life must contend with the current preference of Americans for loose connections and low rates of affiliation.

The malaise of the times was famously captured by Robert Putnam in his landmark *Bowling Alone*, a sweeping analysis of "the collapse and revival of American community." Surveying the broad range of activities in which Americans partake of civic engagement, Putnam concluded that all kinds of association, ranging from political participation to volunteering and philanthropy, to small social connections in the workplace, extended family gatherings, religious groupings and social networks—all were attenuating in the closing decades of the twentieth century. The "social glue" holding Americans together was eroding.

In large measure, this new trend was rooted in the heightened individualism of American society, which enthroned the "sovereign self" as the central authority. In such a climate, mutual responsibility, let alone, obligations have been deemed suspect. Writing in 1985, Robert Bellah and his associates expressed concern that "individualism may have grown cancerous—that it may be destroying those social integuments that…moderate its more destructive potentialities." Still, they were filled with optimism, believing Americans would never tire of being joiners and doers; they would always "get involved." Fifteen years later, Putnam more soberly found a society of Americans who "bowl alone," rather than in leagues, a society lacking in social capital.

American Jews have not been immune to these trends. In their study of moderately affiliated American Jews, Steven M. Cohen and Arnold Eisen determined that for many of these Jews, "the public sphere [of Jewish life] bears the burden of demonstrating its importance to Jewish loyalties nurtured and focused elsewhere." Over 40 percent of respondents to their survey concurred with the statement: "I find Jewish organizations remote and irrelevant to me." Rather than regarding Jewish organizations as a potential "locus for friendship, a place where they could socialize with other Jews in an easy and relaxed atmosphere," many American Jews perceived Jewish organizational life as exploitative, expecting much and giving little in return.

The consequences of this shift in outlook are not difficult to discern. According to the National Jewish Populations Study of 2000-2001, among the population of Jews most engaged with Jewish life (some 4.3 million people), 44 percent claim affiliation with no Jewish institution and an additional 28 percent are affiliated with only one. During the 1990s, membership in Jewish organizations other than synagogues and Jewish Community Centers declined from 31 percent to 24 percent. According to one estimate, the large membership organizations collectively declined in the last decade of the twentieth century from 1.2 million adult members to around 950,000, hardly evidence that American Jews continue to be a community of joiners.

As for voluntarism: one quarter of Jews claimed to engage in voluntary activities for a Jewish cause, as compared to only 18 percent who volunteered for non-sectarian causes. Not surprisingly, volunteering for a Jewish organization was associated with higher levels of Jewish education, attending religious services, in-marriage, raising Jewish children and having friendship circles consisting mainly of other Jews. Based on these patterns, a study of the subject concluded: "As Jewish connections strengthen, volunteering for Jewish organizations become more and more likely, relative to volunteering for non-Jewish organizations." Still, as the large majority of American Jews is gravitating away from Jewish involvement, membership organizations must contend with a dwindling pool of supporters and volunteers.

Similar patterns are at work in the realm of philanthropy. Based on responses to the 1990 National Jewish Population Study, sociologists concluded that 56 percent of American Jews claimed to have donated funds to a Jewish cause in 1989 (compared with 67 percent who claimed to have made a gift to non-Jewish causes). A decade later, virtually the identical percentages of the most Jewishly identified population claimed to have given to a Jewish cause (54.4 percent), but this time the figure excluded at least one million more marginal Jews.

These figures enumerate the giving patterns of all American Jews, but it is well-known that most institutions subsist on large gifts. While it is not possible to gauge precisely how much "big-givers" donate annually, it is estimated that some $30 billion in assets sit in some 9,000 Jewish family foundations. Several studies have demonstrated that only a fraction of these funds make their way to Jewish causes, while the bulk flows to non-sectarian causes.

The populations most likely to volunteer and give to Jewish causes are not randomly distributed within American Jewry. Ample survey data attests to age differences—older populations are far more likely to give and volunteer than are younger ones, with the sharpest drop off among those in their twenties and thirties; area of residence—the further Jewish families live from centers of Jewish concentration, the less likely they are to participate; regional variations—Jews in the Northeast and Midwest are most likely to be joiners and donors, whereas Jews in the West and in sunbelt communities are least likely to affiliate. Social networks also play a role: having Jewish friends correlates strongly with participation. Above all, marital patterns are the most critical factor: in-married Jews are far more likely than the inter-married and the non-married to contribute and volunteer. The collective efforts of the American Jews on behalf of their own are largely dependent today on a population that is fading from the scene—and many Jewish organizations already are struggling under the strain.

Finally, the political orientation of American Jewish organizations continues to operate in a time warp, fighting the battles of yesteryear, while current needs go unanswered. In contrast to 1938 and even 1948, American Jews are not victims of exclusion. They have won the battle against discrimination. They have allies in many quarters, including the most unlikely ones. Who could have imagined seventy years ago that evangelical Christians would be staunch supporters of Israel? Who could have imagined that Catholics and conservative Protestants would have sought alliances with Jews to strengthen religion in this country? But Jews continue to regard these groups with suspicion, if not hostility. They are deeply concerned that those groups will try to convert their children, a remarkable fear considering that hundreds of thousands of children born to Jewish parents in interfaith marriages are already on their way to becoming Christians.

Rather than seeking political alliances and public policies that would strengthen collective Jewish existence in this country, Jewish organizations continue to behave as if we are still back in 1938, battling a non-existent discrimination, while ignoring symptoms of internal decay.

Let me illustrate this point about our public policy stances with the following anecdote that brought home to me how strange the thinking of individual Jews has become. Last year I met with someone I had not seen in a number of years and naturally we compared notes. She spoke with pride about her daughter, a bright, attractive woman completing her doctorate at one of the most prestigious universities in the land. She happily told me that her daughter has been actively involved with Jewish life through her teens and twenties, and hoped to marry and have a number of children. But she also noted that her daughter was not dating Jewish men; indeed she expected her daughter either to marry a non-Jew and have a few children or to have a single child on her own. When I asked my acquaintance how she felt about this, she calmly accepted that this is how things are today. The conversation then meandered and shortly before parting, current events came up. My acquaintance expressed her fury at what is happening to the U.S. Supreme Court, speaking with great passion about the impending ratification of Judge Alito. This topic really evoked her passionate feelings.

As we parted ways, I could not help but think that our conversation neatly captured in microcosm what I consider so bizarre in American Jewish public life. The imagined changes the revamped Supreme Court might countenance—now there is an issue to get ourselves worked up about! But that our own Jewish children remain single in high numbers, that those who marry do not bear children at replacement level, and that huge percentages who do have children do not raise them as Jews—that's just the way things are. No point examining how we created this mess or whether there is anything the Jewish community might do to address it. It's no one's business. Better that we should get exercised about the Supreme Court!

The implosion of Jewish life ought to be the primary business item on communal and personal agendas. To sum up: our numbers are bound to decline; allegiance to the needs of the Jewish people cannot be assumed; and instead of focusing on our internal problems, we focus on the world at large. We seem bereft of worthy Jewish causes. Those Jews who do identify are withdrawing into ever smaller communities and have lost a sense of connection to a larger Jewish purpose.

IV

So how do we save American Jews?

First, let me state what must cease: the efforts to silence healthy debate. In 1938 and into the Holocaust, much of the leadership of the American Jewish community was silenced by its fears of anti-Semitism and charges of disloyalty to America. These related fears obstructed an effective political response by the American Jewish community to the Holocaust. Today our leadership is again silenced, but this time by fears that it will alienate constituencies. Don't talk about intermarriage because you will antagonize intermarried Jews and their extended families; don't talk about declining birthrates because young people don't want to hear of it. A half a year ago, I attended a session on Jewish peoplehood in which a twenty-something warned Jewish leaders: "Don't talk to us about babies. We don't want to hear of it." Sha-shtill.

And then there is the silencing of those who point to declining Jewish engagement and connection to the Jewish people. Don't talk about these things: they demoralize; the young people don't want to hear of it; and the rest of the community will get upset. And so today we have a new kind of Marrano: Jewish leaders who will privately admit that they don't believe the happy talk they mouth in public. Sha-shtill.

Some of the same people who stormed the federation General Assembly in 1969, bemoaning the skewed priorities of the time, are now the most avid proponents of the sha- shtill mode. Back then, they had no inhibitions about ruffling the feathers of the establishment; but today as they have become the establishment they live in fear of challenging the community and shaking up Jewish organizations. Whereas once young Jews confronted the Jewish establishment for covering up, today in their middle age years they participate in a cover-up—all in the name of pluralism, big tents, political correctness, and "I'm ok, you're ok." Sha shtill.

And as for religious and ideological differences: whereas American Jews in the first half of the twentieth century bitterly contested Zionism and later engaged in religious disputes, today they tend to withdraw into their own small sub-communities. Better that we should ignore those with whom we disagree than contend with them. So Jews of different religious movements avoid one another, rather than argue. Jews who disagree about Israel retreat into their own camps, hearing only views congruent with their own. And everyone feels virtuous because they are so civil. I recently asked a prominent leader of the Reform movement how it is that the Religious Action Center of the Reform movement can espouse extreme positions, such as its call for immediate withdrawal from Iraq. "Are there no Republicans left in the Reform movement?" I asked. The answer I got back was "sure there are folks in the Reform movement who oppose the official line. But the religion of Reform is civility." Better that they should keep their mouths shut, rather than engage in dispute. Sha-shtill.

That is a luxury we cannot afford--precisely because it is not 1938. We are not a community poised for growth, as we were seventy years ago. We are a shrinking community. We are not a community ripping itself apart over Jewish causes; we are a community bereft of causes. We are not a community under siege to anti-Semites, but a community facing grave internal problems and our politics has not caught up with those realities. So we are in urgent need of more debate, not less.

Second, and very much related to this stifling of open discussion, we are a community that no longer can afford to substitute process for content. If only we process questions properly, many seem to believe, we can all stay together. If only we work in a pluralistic fashion and never give offense to any Jew, we will win back large numbers of the disaffected. If only our Jewish organizations would behave like "big tents," they would once again attract wide-scale support. That, too, is a delusion. Sure we ought to be hospitable; sure we have to strengthen our ground rules for engaging in controversies; and sure we ought to open many doors to Jews to create portals of entry into Jewish life. But once we get those Jews into the door, what do we want to share with them? What is the content of Judaism we wish to impart in our Jewish schools? What is the policy our synagogues will formulate? What do our organizations stand for? Without addressing questions of content, we will quickly lose the Jews who have entered our doors as they quickly discover how impoverished we are, how little we stand for.

And third, let's move beyond the delusion that Tikkun Olam ("mending the world") is a cure-all. There is ample reason to work on improving life on this earth. Like other decent human beings, we have a responsibility to bring succor to the weak and needy, resist injustice, and care for our planet. But one does not have to be Jewish to do good deeds. The calls for ever more universalism may attract some Jews to participate in an organized Jewish effort to do good, but it will not keep them for long. Habitat for Humanity, Cancer Care, the United Way and a myriad of other non-sectarian agencies also do good. We have to match our calls for

Tikkun Olam with education about the importance and value of Tikkun Am Yisrael. We must balance universal concern with looking after our own, not only the downtrodden but also the large swathe of Jews in this country who deserve to participate in an enriching, dynamic, meaningful Jewish enterprise.

Let's start by talking to our young people. It is sobering to reflect on the shift that has been wrought since the 1960s. Then young Jews rallied in the hundreds of thousands for Israel and freeing Soviet Jewry. Then they stormed the General Assembly of the federations to demand greater investment in Jewish education, rather than support of non-sectarian causes. Today many of our twenty- and thirty-somethings demand more universalism and ridicule those concerned about Jewish needs. I know because I have been the object of such ridicule. Just recently, for example, in an online blog published in Ha'aretz, a young fellow unburdened himself as follows:

> For Wertheimer and Cohen (my co-author), whose article in *Commentary* published last year wails against our plummeting ethnic identity, the apparent crisis can be summed up by the observation that American Jews seem to have more time for the people of Darfur than their own people. Shocking! In other words, as long as we can convince this wayward new crop of Jews that delivering groceries to a senior center—a Jewish senior center!—is of more moral importance than preventing the mass-rape of eleven-year-old girls, everything is going to be just fine.

Leaving aside the caricature of what we had actually written, there remains the perception that Jewish needs are secondary to the needs of others. Once upon a time, critics of the Jewish community resisted the obsession with universal causes at the expense of Jewish ones. Writing in 1964, Rabbi Harold Schulweis disparaged the "flagrant inconsistency" of Jewish liberals who were normally impassioned defenders of every group except for the Jews. In the same year, Rabbi Arthur Hertzberg observed that democracy can become a form of totalitarianism when it demands a leveling. He asked, "Is the primary purpose of the Jewish community to help itself disappear, or is it to help itself survive? What is the meaning of Jewish survival?" I cite these two examples because both statements were made by men of the Left. Where are their counterparts today? Lamentably, today's so-called "progressive" Jews now demand less attention to Jewish needs, rather than an intensification of efforts to enrich and deepen Jewish life.

If we reversed these unhealthy current tendencies, we might have a chance to build a community that:

1. Takes Jewish issues seriously and welcomes healthy debate. As the anthropologist Barbara Meyerhoff wrote, "anger is a form of social cohesion and a strong and reliable one. To fight with each other, people must share norms, rules, vocabulary and knowledge. Fighting is a partnership requiring cooperation." Rather than stifle healthy debate, we should encourage it. We might actually make some progress in developing new approaches to our difficult challenges. And we might stimulate more people to join organized Jewish life, rather than stay away.

2. Creates communities of content and not only of process. The clearer we are about what we stand for, the greater the likelihood Jews will be prepared to sacrifice and volunteer because they will find engagement meaningful rather than bland. Today our parve (neutral) organizations fail to grab people by the lapels.

3. Realizes that the greatest challenge is not winning acceptance by the larger society, but helping Jews appreciate the virtues of Jewish distinctiveness and particularity. Enough of all the talk about how congruent Judaism is with today's right-thinking outlook. Enough with the efforts to fit in. We are not living in 1938 when society pressured Jews to conform. Enough of all the talk about how Jews are like everyone else –only more so; that Judaism is perfectly in sync with the prevailing mood; and that Jewish holidays are so wonderful because they express the universal longing of all human beings. Let's shout from the rooftops that to be Jewish means to view the world through a distinctive set of spectacles. Let's announce that for all our openness to the world at large, we regard Jewish civilization as rich and stimulating on its own terms. And let's understand on a deep level that the challenge of our time is not winning acceptance from our neighbors—we won that battle—but embracing what our ancestors lived and died for: the belief that to be Jewish is to be different.

11

1938 as Paradigm

Lawrence Grossman

In his chapter on "Saving American Jewry," Professor Jack Wertheimer paints a bleak picture of the American Jewish condition.

He begins, to be sure, with good news, cataloging the ways in which the quality of Jewish life in America today is far better than it was in 1938. After noting the postwar changes in American society that opened the way for Jews to achieve a degree of economic and social success unprecedented in Jewish history, Wertheimer focuses on three significant substantive changes within American Jewish life that have immeasurably strengthened its collective identity:

1. A renewed sense of Jewish peoplehood, stimulated by the success of Zionism and the creation of the State of Israel in 1948.
2. The revitalization of Orthodox Judaism—which appeared doomed to obsolescence in 1938—both numerically and in terms of communal influence.
3. A renaissance of serious Jewish education, based primarily on the proliferation of Jewish day schools, but encompassing as well adult education, university Jewish studies programs, and all sorts of informal Jewish educational ventures.

Despite these achievements, Wertheimer warns, American Jewry is in grave danger of erosion. The very openness of American life and the individualistic nature of contemporary culture place at risk Jewish group identity. In pursuit of individual material success and psychic self-fulfillment, Jews are, all too often, staying single longer and marrying later, and choosing non-Jewish marriage partners, choices that produce fewer

Jewish children. And as boundaries between Jew and non-Jew fade, Jews become caught up in universalistic causes. All these trends vitiate the sense of Jewish peoplehood, leaving relatively few—other than the Orthodox and those with the most extensive Jewish educations—who maintain strong Jewish identity.

The "Wertheimer Thesis," which its author has previously formulated in other contexts, has generated criticism from those who believe that American Jewish life, despite its deviations from traditional conceptions of Jewishness, is at least as strong as ever; those who see universalistic causes as the only way the Jewish community can attract the allegiance of young people; and those who suspect that Wertheimer's agenda is to sacrifice individual autonomy (especially that of Jewish women) on the altar of larger families.

These criticisms, I believe, are misplaced, as they evade the central challenge that Wertheimer presents—that strong Jewish group identity, without which there has never been a successful Jewish community anywhere—cannot coexist with limitless autonomy of the kind available to us today.

Nevertheless, Wertheimer errs in framing the discussion in a Holocaust context, for example, decrying "a paralysis quite similar to that suffered by our forebears seventy years ago," and condemning "Shah-shtill" Jewish leaders who "silence debate" as did their predecessors in 1938, though this time not about Hitler, but about the demographic dangers to Jewish life. He has, perhaps, been seduced by the theme of this volume, "Is It 1938 Again?' to stretch our subject, the spiritual and cultural health of the Jewish community, onto the procrustean bed of the tragic historical events that led to the destruction of six million of our people.

The historical cycles of Jewish creativity do not necessarily match the chronological patterns that mark our confrontations with anti-Semitism. The lack of such congruence is especially glaring in our case: the disaster of 1938–1945, after all, occurred thousands of miles away from the area of our concern, the United States.

Indeed, looking back from the perspective of seven decades, 1938 was a very good year for American Jewry. Rather than engaging in Holocaust metaphors, those who are intent today on "saving" the Jewish community might want to look at that year more closely, for it turns out that the seeds of each of Wertheimer's three pillars of postwar Jewish achievement—peoplehood, Orthodoxy, and Jewish education—were already planted and beginning to grow in 1938.

Zionism and Peoplehood

For Reform Jews—members of the largest, most successful, and most Americanized element of the Jewish community—Jewish peoplehood was a subject of considerable controversy during 1938. The year before, in May 1937, "obscured by the ominous international situation," as one Jewish periodical put it, the Central Conference of American Rabbis (CCAR), Reform's rabbinic body, voted to repudiate its anti-Zionist tradition and espouse Jewish peoplehood.

Until 1937, the official line of Reform, adopted by the CCAR at its convention in Pittsburgh in 1885, presented Judaism as "the highest conception of the God-idea"—that is, as a spiritual system with no ethnic component. Religious ritual, for the "Pittsburgh Platform," was "altogether foreign to our present mental and spiritual state." As a religious rather a national community that aspired to universal justice and peace, Reform Jews did not expect "a return to Palestine."

Meeting in Columbus, Ohio in 1937, the Reform rabbis reversed its position and declared that "Judaism in the soul of which Israel is the body," recognized the "group-loyalty" of secular Jews, posited that "Judaism is a way of life" with significant "customs, symbols, and ceremonies," and favored "the rehabilitation of Palestine," including the "obligation of all Jewry to aid in its upbuilding as a Jewish homeland...."

By no means did the "Columbus Platform" end the debate within Reform Judaism over Zionism and peoplehood; some adherents of what became known as Classical Reform continued to deny that Judaism had a national component. But the coming of World War II and the dire need for a Jewish homeland to take in refugees quickly made that position obsolete. The founding of the schismatic American Council for Judaism by anti-Zionist Reform Jews a few years later indicated that the anti-Zionists had lost the battle for control of their movement.

By 1938, then, the "Zionization" of the most significant and least traditional branch of American Jewry was well underway, and with it, the recognition of Jewish peoplehood by the broader American Jewish community.

Orthodoxy Awakens

Orthodoxy, in 1938, was widely perceived as an immigrant form of Judaism that was fated to die out with the older generation. American Jews who sought to perpetuate the traditional Jewish way of life were attracted to the Conservative movement, which taught the adaptation of

Jewish practices to American mores. However, a little-noticed event that year presaged the phenomenal explosion of Orthodoxy that would later take observers by surprise.

The year 1938 marked the fiftieth anniversary of the B. Manischewitz Company, based in Cincinnati, which produced matzo. To commemorate the occasion, the Union of Orthodox Rabbis (Agudath Harabanim), the rabbinic body of the East-European-born, Yiddish-speaking, unaccul-turated rabbis, held a meeting before Passover to lavish praise on the company. It also published a list of hundreds of rabbis who endorsed Manischewitz matzos as kosher to eat on Passover.

For a century, in fact, since the first use of machine-made matzot in France, their kosher-for-Passover status had been a matter of controversy. Some rabbinic authorities had banned them, insisting that only hand-made matzot were acceptable. For many of the more conservative rabbis, the unacceptability of machine matzot had less to do with purely legal concerns than with the fear that innovation of any kind in the practice of Jewish law could open the floodgates to the collapse of tradition—the view first articulated, in a different context, by Rabbi Moshe Sofer in the early nineteenth century, that anything new is forbidden by the Torah. Machine matzot, therefore, although widely consumed, remained suspect in many Orthodox circles.

The address of Rabbi Joseph Konvitz, president of the Union of Ortho-dox Rabbis, at the 1938 commemorative event for Manischewitz was thus of great significance. Before movingly bemoaning the plight of European Jewry under the shadow of Nazism, he noted that whereas, in previous generations, the kashrut of hand matzo was certain while that of the ma-chine product was questionable, "today the opposite is true: the kashrut of the machine is certain and that of 'the hands' is questionable."

This public repudiation of Luddite notions dismissive of innova-tion—hardly noticed outside strictly Orthodox precincts at the time—was a harbinger of things to come. In the postwar decades, American Ortho-doxy would prove its attraction for younger Jews precisely through the adaptation of modern techniques to spread ancient truths: clever use of the print, audio, and electronic media; sophisticated political activity that builds coalitions both within and outside the Jewish community; keen understanding of the spiritual hunger that would transform the American religious landscape; and the production of original works in literate English, as well as translations of Jewish classics, published in aesthetically attractive form.

The New Jewish Day School

To appreciate the significance of the year 1938 for Jewish education in the United States—and particularly for the development of the day school—one must first note the findings of a special article that appeared in the American Jewish Year Book for 1936–37, written by the educational director of the Jewish Educational Association of New York.

It found that less than a quarter of Jewish elementary school-age children, in New York and nationally, were getting any Jewish education, and that the great majority of these dropped out after a few years. Furthermore, the Jewish education referred to was supplementary: one or more days a week after public-school hours and/or Sunday. (There was barely any secondary Jewish education to speak of.) The small number of elementary day schools then operating—which, the author points out, were commonly called "parochial" schools—were mostly "the old type Yeshibah" with secular classes added on. As for the few modernized day schools, he believed they "must always remain the opportunity of the exclusive few." It was taken for granted that the Jewish love affair with the American public school would last forever.

Although no one knew it at the time, it was the 1937–38 school year that witnessed the "takeoff" of the Jewish day school in two strategic communities. That year in New York, Rabbi Joseph H. Lookstein created the Ramaz School, and in Boston, Rabbi Joseph B. Soloveitchik created the Maimonides School, each starting with a small class of first-graders. Both men were far-sighted Orthodox rabbis who managed to garner the support of lay people who were largely not observant Jews, and would not send their own children to the new schools. And both recognized that to succeed in the battle for Jewish affections with the public school, an American day-school education had to provide excellence in both the religious and the secular curricula.

This was an omen of things to come: "The 1940's marked the period of phenomenal growth of the Jewish day schools." Gradually, the fear that day-school education could ghettoize Jewish youngsters would dissipate, and by the beginning of the twenty-first century attendance at day school had become not only an Orthodox imperative, but a live option among Conservative and Reform Jews as well, forming the basis for the current great surge of interest in Jewish education of all types.

A Lesson from 1938

In full awareness of the ominous Nazi shadow that hovered over millions of European Jews, American Jewry created the mechanisms for a revival of Jewish life: a commitment to peoplehood, a form of religious Orthodoxy that embodied authentic tradition while utilizing the most up-to-date techniques, and the model of a Jewish day school that offered serious Jewish education without sacrificing broad and deep training in the arts and sciences.

Whether or not the threats that now confront the Jewish people worldwide turn out to parallel those of 1938, there is no warrant to invoke the Holocaust in criticizing the shortcomings of American Jewish life that Wertheimer chronicles so well. Decades hence, scholars looking back at 2007 may well detect the beginnings of yet another Jewish revival. Of course we cannot know for sure, but, since all of Jewish history has been punctuated by unexpected and unaccountable triumphs, I would not bet against it.

Notes

1.   See the letters from readers in *Commentary* (October 2006), pp. 4–6, 8, 10, 12, 14, in response to Steven M. Cohen and Jack Wertheimer, "Whatever Happened to the Jewish People?" that appeared in the issue of June 2006, pp. 33–37.

2.   Editorial in the *Reconstructionist* 3 (October 8, 1937), p. 6.

3.   Dana Evan Kaplan, *American Reform Judaism: An Introduction* (New Brunswick, NJ: Rutgers University Press, 2003), pp. 45–49.

4.   Ibid., pp. 49–51. A useful comparative chart of the various Reform platforms can be found in the unpaginated supplement to Eugene B. Borowitz, *Reform Judaism Today: How We Live* (New York: Behrman House, 1978).

5.   Material about the Manischewitz anniversary takes up much of the March 1938 issue of the Hebrew monthly *Hapardes*, which was the organ of the Union of Orthodox Rabbis.

6.   Meir Hildesheimer and Yehoshua Lieberman, "The Controversy Surrounding Machine-Made Matzot: Halakhic, Social, and Economic Repercussions," *Hebrew Union College Annual* 75 (2004), pp. 193–262; and Chaim Gartner, "'Machine Matzot': The Halakhic Controversy as a Means of Defining Orthodox Identity," in Yosef Salmon, Aviezer Ravitzky, and Adam Ferziger, eds., *Orthodox Judaism: New Views* (Jerusalem: Magnes Press, 2006; in Hebrew), pp. 395–425. On the significance of Manischewitz see Jonathan D. Sarna, "How Matzah Became Square: Manischewitz and the Development of Machine-Made Matzah in the United States, Victor Selmanowitz Lecture," pamphlet (New York: Touro College, 2005).

7.   "Ceremony of the Baking of 'Shemurah Matzo' at the Manischewitz Factory," Hapardes (March 1938), p. 5.

8.   Israel Chipkin, "Twenty-Five Years of Jewish Education in the United States," *American Jewish Year Book* 1936–37, Vol. 38 (Philadelphia, PA: Jewish Publication Society of America, 1936), pp. 27–116. Day schools are discussed on pp. 55–59.

9. Jeffrey S. Gurock, "The Ramaz Version of American Orthodoxy," in Gurock, ed., *Ramaz: School, Community, Scholarship, and Orthodoxy* (Hoboken, NJ: Ktav, 1989), p. 40: Seth Farber, *An American Orthodox Dreamer: Rabbi Joseph B. Soloveitchik and Boston's Maimonides School* (Hanover, MA: Brandeis University Press/ University Press of New England, 2004), p. 49.

10. Judah Pilch, "From the Early Forties to the Mid-Sixties," in Pilch, ed., *A History of Jewish Education in the United States* (New York: American Association for Jewish Education, 1969), p. 140.

11. Jack Wertheimer, "Jewish Education in the United States: Recent Trends and Issues," *American Jewish Year Book* 1999, Vol. 99 (New York: American Jewish Committee, 1999), pp. 52–57.

12

From Hatred to Love: Is it Good—or Bad—for the Jews?

Samuel C. Heilman

As one who is both a child of Holocaust survivors and born in Germany just after the end of Nazi rule, I have always grown up in the shadow of the question that serves as the theme of this conference, sensitive to the possibility that Jewish continuity might be threatened by some sinister force not recognized in its incipiency. So much of my parents' history and the history of their generation were after all marked by the fact that they and so many Jews like them did not sufficiently realize the extent of the threats of 1938. As part of the Orthodox community in Eastern Europe, they had, alas, followed the very bad advice of most of their religious leaders who had warned against leaving the Jewish world of Europe for either the *trefe medina*, as America was sometimes called, or the Zionist heresy of the *yishuv* in the land of Israel. In both these places, most of the Orthodox rabbis argued, Jews might physically survive but Judaism would not. Had more Jews *not* heeded their advice and left for these two places—when it was still possible to do so—six million might not have perished.

But were the rabbis correct? Are America and today's Israel places where Jews survive but Judaism does not? The verdict is mixed. At least in America, this is both the best of times and the worst of times for Judaism. This has been a time when American Jews have experienced a minimum of prejudice, when almost all domains of life have been opened to them (so much so that diminishing numbers of them care to engage in

99

strictly Jewish activities, from being teachers of Jewish subjects to being fundraisers for Jewish causes). This has also been a time of extraordinary assimilation, of swelling rates of intermarriage and of large numbers of people simply ignoring their Jewishness completely. America often loves Jews to death in its enveloping embrace; the Gentiles love us so much they want to marry us—and we them. Jews have embraced all the opportunity open to them, regardless of the cost to Jewish distinctiveness. Not only in America, but even in Israel, the desire to be part of modern Western civilization and popular culture is perhaps stronger among most Jews than the desire to remain attached to ancient traditions and parochial Jewish identities. The road to Jerusalem today is marked by the giant golden arches of MacDonald's in the mall at the edge of the city, and in the pages of the *New York Times Magazine* a graduate of an American Orthodox day school, who teaches at Harvard, celebrates his intermarriage to a non-Jewish Korean-American.

Ironically, this is a time when, except for the ultra-Orthodox, Jews have become largely indistinguishable from non-Jews—certainly when compared to some of the other more recent unmeltable ethnics. Indeed, since so many of us are married to non-Jews, we are far more part of the American fabric than ever before.

This is a time when American Jewish physical safety is unparalleled in history (except perhaps by those few ultra-Orthodox who still live in inner city neighborhoods like Crown Heights, Brooklyn) but Jewish cultural integrity seems more precarious than ever before. This is a time when the Jewish population of America is steadily diminishing in numbers, certainly relative to the general American population. And it is a time when Israel, though militarily strong, finds powerful adversaries committing themselves to "wiping it off the map," while in the United Nations more than sixty-five condemning resolutions have been offered against it.

This is a time when Jews have no trouble building synagogues, but they have all sorts of trouble filling them. This is a time when the number of young Jews who affiliate with established Jewish denominations shrinks. This has been a time when the quality of Jewish education for those who receive it is perhaps higher than ever before in history and, the output of Jewish scholarship, whether in the yeshivas or in university Jewish studies programs, is overwhelming in its scope and amplitude. Never before in America has so much Judaica been published or have there been more universities where Jewish studies are taught. But it is also a time when most American Jews receive the most minimal level of such education, a time when a majority of these who constitute the People of the Book do not read the great books of Jewish life, and even if they wanted to, most could neither read nor comprehend the great corpus of Jewish literature in its Hebrew (or Aramaic) original. Along with the many cultural islands populated by prodigious Jewish scholars there is a surrounding sea of those who are Jewish illiterates.

This is a time in America when there is no shame in being a Jew and yet fewer American Jews seem to know what being a Jew means. This is a time when American Jews can and do marvel at the accomplishments of a Jewish state in Israel, but when less than half of them have ever visited it and practically none of them would even entertain the thought of living there. This is a time when Jewish wealth and power reaches into the corridors of American power and influence, when Jewish money endows symphony orchestras, art museums, and major universities, but the number of those who work for the Jewish community or give to Jewish causes shrinks daily. This is a time when many who care about Jewish education have sent their children to day schools and yeshivas, but few if any of those people actually provide the personnel of Jewish education. This *is* the best of times and the worst of times.

Those who have argued that Israel is the answer forget that among our young, Israel no longer represents the Promised Land. Not only do they care more about America, as Dr. Wertheimer has suggested, but increasingly they do *not* care about Israel, and more and more they see Israel as the incarnation of malevolence or a pale version of America. To be sure, these feelings have risen along with the intermarriage rate. And of course, what we find overwhelming among American Jews is the abysmal ignorance of things Jewish by the vast majority, even greater among the young than those of my generation.

But these dangers are not precisely the same ones of 1938. Does that mean that today's threats are less worrisome? I think not. History does not repeat itself in precisely the same way. Each generation must find the means necessary to provide for its own survival. One can only hope that this one will find both the will and the tools necessary for the task.

13

Facing Armageddon—
Evangelicals and the Jews

Yechiel Eckstein

The cryptic title of my chapter, "Facing Armageddon: Evangelicals and the Jews," leaves lots of space to maneuver, especially within the overall context of the conference theme. I would like to divide my comments into two parts: the first will accommodate the sponsors of this outstanding conference by specifically addressing my assigned topic; and the second will address the broader conference theme, namely how ought we to relate to evangelicals when Jewish survival is at stake.

The basic origin of the term "Armageddon" is the corruption of the Hebrew words *Har Megiddo*, that is Mount Megiddo, which if you repeat it quickly—"Ar Megiddo ... Armeggedo..."—it comes out eventually as "Armageddon." The scenario known as "Armageddon" is described in the Book of Daniel in our *Tanach* (the Old Testament) and in the Book of Revelation in the New Testament. These accounts depict the final battle between Good and Evil, when the destruction will be so great, says the New Testament, that the blood of the victims will reach the horses' bridles. Actually, we find a very similar, though not as illustrative, account in Jewish belief describing the final battle between Gog and Magog, the death of Messiah, son of Joseph, and the coming of Messiah, son of David, who will bring redemption to its conclusion.

Virtually every Western religion, including Judaism, has a number of stories and versions of what will happen "in end times" as it is called, or the *eschaton*, the end of days scenario. (This concept reflects not a cyclical view of time, as Eastern religions have, but a linear one with a distinct beginning and end.) Insomuch as we Jews are part of Christian and Muslim eschatology, it behooves us to explore the subject. But we should not give it more credence than it deserves. Nor should we skip over the question of what role an eschatological vision or an apocalyptic future plays in our overall ethos, what impact on the here and now it has, and what actions we must take or not take. In short, the key question is what theological framework do we put around the world's future – and ours? Put differently, is the best-selling *Left Behind* series just pleasant science fiction, or is it a road map of how believers feel they should face the end of days?

For example, we Jews have our own eschatology: history as we know it will come to an end, with the coming of *mashiach* (Messiah), the judgment of all human beings, the ingathering of the Jewish people, a period of suffering (*chevlai mashiach*), the restoration of Israel, and the fulfillment of prophetic promises, such as "Nation shall not lift up sword..." and "The desert will bloom like a rose." At that juncture we will also rediscover the lost tribes of Israel and bring them to the Land of Israel. And, of course, part of the Jewish eschatology is also the battle between Gog and Magog.

It is important to point out that as crucial as our eschatology is, it does not necessarily speak to or inform, let alone dictate, how we act in the here and now, particularly toward other groups who do not share our views. For example, the prophets spoke at length about *kibbutz galuyot*, the ingathering of the exiles. Today, I and millions of others have moved to Israel. Indeed, we help others do so. The International Fellowship of Christians and Jews (IFCJ) has enabled hundreds of thousands of Jews all over the world to go on *aliyah*—immigrate to Israel—through the Jewish Agency. We have contributed well over $100 million for this purpose in recent years, all from Christians seeking to bless Israel and her people. But what guides and motivates the Israeli government as it promotes *aliyah* is not the idea that messiah will then come sooner, as much as other factors such as freedom, Zionism, demography, and helping Jews escape anti-Semitism. Even Orthodox Jews who believe we are living in "the beginning of the sprouting of our redemption" (as the Chief Rabbinate has declared) do not promote *aliyah* for this reason. In short, it is possible to look at the miracle of the birth of Israel and *aliyah* from around the world as the fulfillment of prophecies speaking of end times. But no one I know supports *aliyah* or Israel for this reason, namely that Mashiach will thereby come sooner, even if they believe that it is an ultimate consequence. The Jewish eschatology does give a theological framework of *"acharit hayamin"* end times. But while it demands *tikun olam,* improving the world, it does not—and was never intended to—prompt eschatologically driven *actions*. The same is true of Christian eschatology. We need to look at Christian eschatology not as something motivating the actions of Christians, as in perceiving a need to kill all the infidels so as to bring all people to Christian faith, but as giving a theological framework.

My own experience is the following: The Fellowship raised roughly $75 million in 2006 from over half a million people, mostly Christian donors. We receive over 3,000 pieces of mail a day. And in over twenty-five years since I founded this organization I don't recall getting even one gift or letter of support stating that they are acting in order so that their eschatological scenario would unfold. Do many of them believe in the scenario? Yes, I'm sure. But that does not lead them to take action that will bring about such a scenario. What I'm saying, then, is that the common perception—declared by people who have never even read the New Testament or the Book of Revelation but somehow consider themselves experts on why Evangelicals support Israel – is bogus from beginning to end. And it is amazing how many Jews and journalists believe and print this stuff as if it is gospel, so to speak, without knowing what on earth they're talking about. In fact, it is pure fiction.

A few years ago, we at IFCJ commissioned a study by the Terrence Group for the purpose of scientifically assessing American non-Jews' attitudes towards Israel. As we all know, Evangelicals have a higher support rate. Why? The vast majority gave a non theological reason – because of the shared values of democracy, Judeo-Christian ethics and freedom that the U.S. and Israel are committed to. But even when pushed to give *theological* reasons for their support, the vast majority cited the biblical verse in Genesis 12:3 where God promises Abraham, "I will bless those who bless you..."

Evangelicals believe in our bible, the *Tanach*, often taking it literally. And Jews in that bible are G-d's Chosen people whom they, gentiles, are commanded to help as Isaiah declared, "Comfort ye, comfort ye my people." Therefore, the stereotype believed so ubiquitously – that the only reason Evangelicals support Israel is so that all Jews will return there, accept Jesus or die – is propaganda, bogus *nahreshkeit*. Armageddon plays little, if any, role in their support for Israel and the Jewish people.

Let me cite another example. The Fellowship raises millions of dollars each year from Christians to help elderly Jews in the Ukraine, Russia, Uzbekistan, and dozens of other poverty-stricken countries in the former Soviet Union. Annually, we give millions of dollars to provide food, heating fuel, medicine and more for these Jewish people. And no one has any expectations that these elderly people will move to Israel, accept Jesus, and such. Our Christian donors contribute gladly and sacrificially out of a genuine love for Israel and the Jewish people, one motivated by their belief in God and the Bible. Their goal? To bless G-d's chosen people and be thereby blessed. Their motivation has nothing whatsoever to do with Armageddon or their eschatology as a whole.

While it is true that theological views can indeed spill over into diabolical action, that is not necessarily what happens. As we have seen, in the example of Judaism and Christianity—I cannot comment on Islam, since I have no expertise in that subject—there is a major disconnect between what their followers may believe will happen in the end of days, and what motivates them to do what they do today.

Take President Bush. As everyone knows, he is an evangelical Christian. Does anyone really think the reason he stands with Israel is eschatological so as to bring Armageddon? Nonsense—and pretty frightening if it were true. On the other hand, take a look at Islam, particularly through the eyes of the president of Iran—where the nexus between eschatological belief, expectations and action is very real and very direct. These Shi'a Islamists are eagerly expecting the imminent arrival of the twelfth Imam, the *Mahdi* or messiah, who will destroy Israel. They also believe and are motivated to action now by a very specific predicted scenario, and are therefore actively developing missiles, a nuclear program, and terrorism.

My point is this: Jewish suspicions of evangelical support for Israel, as motivated by Armageddon and ultimately a threat to Jewish life, are really a feeble attempt by the Left to undermine the integrity and importance of evangelical support for Israel. It is, pure and simple, a convenient stereotype which, like other stereotypes, has some basis in fact but is totally devoid of truth. It's a convenient excuse for rejecting an alliance with evangelicals. And it is a view proposed by folks who are, for the most part, ignorant of the evangelical community and what makes them tick, and totally unaware of evangelical theology and eschatology and the role they play in the ethos of individual Christians. In fact, I am certain that these Jews have never actually engaged in a dialogue with an evangelical Christian to discuss the matter and hear their views directly. Perhaps the whole subject of Armageddon can be summed up in the by now well-known anecdote in which Messiah comes and calls a press conference. A journalist asks "Is this your first or second coming?" and the whole world waits for the answer as to who was right all these millennia. The answer Messiah undoubtedly gives to this earth-shattering question is the ironic, enigmatic response: *"no comment."*

However, the subject of how evangelicals view Armageddon and end days needs to be addressed in the larger context of the important overall theme of this book, "Is it 1938 again?" And so, instead of spending more time slaying the dinosaur that doesn't exist, let me address the subject of real importance, namely, evangelicals and how they relate to the question of "Is it 1938 Again?" Incidentally, my response to this question is an emphatic *"Yes."* I believe Israel and the Jewish people are today threatened to a degree we have not experienced since 1938. We are facing an existential threat that can affect the lives of millions of Jews and the future of the State of Israel and the continuity of Judaism. And, I believe, our future as Jews depends heavily on our relationship with our only stalwart friends – America and the world evangelical community.

These devout Christians—some 60 million in the U.S. and hundreds of millions around the world—are today not only not our adversaries, but are our best friends and closest allies. As was once said, the Bible Belt is Israel's safety belt. These are people who will travel on a tour to Israel when others are afraid to visit, contribute money to Israel when others boycott her, promote Israel's good public relations when others attack her. They are people who would literally risk their lives if necessary to help Jews—I am convinced of it. The fact is that philo-Semitism, and particularly Christian theology supporting Jews and Israel, predates Falwell, Robertson, and Hagee. Already in 1891 here in the U.S., William Blackstone, a Christian evangelical, organized a petition signed by a U.S. Supreme Court Justice, the Speaker of the House and J. P. Morgan, calling upon America to restore Palestine for G-d's Chosen people, the Jews. A similar sentiment existed in Great Britain, where there had long been a strong current of Christian Zionism.

And while we can debate beliefs, the bottom line is this: will all the theological positions find expression in corresponding deeds and actions? What will evangelicals do or not do for Israel at this critical time? Of course, the notion of righteous gentiles is not a new one. It can be found in the Talmud and even at the Holocaust museum Yad Vashem, with its "Avenue of the Righteous Gentiles" exhibit, where trees have been planted in honor of those non-Jews who risked or gave their lives to save Jews in the *Shoah*. Today, there are millions of righteous gentiles —Christians who are willing to stand with us in the face of all sorts of threats and dangers to ensure our survival. After thirty years working with them, I am absolutely convinced that if we Jews were ever threatened we would witness the emergence of the Corrie ten Booms, the Oscar Schindlers, the villagers of Le Chambon (an evangelical town in France of 5,000 people who saved an equal number of Jews), and so on. But the key point is that if you believe as I do that this is indeed 1938, then it is essential for us Jews to forge strategic alliances with others. We did not do that in the 1930s. We dare not make that mistake again.

Yet, the organized Jewish community in America is failing drastically in this respect and is, instead, pushing away our best friends. We dare not alienate our natural allies for no good reason. In fact, as Israeli prime ministers since Menachem Begin have said to and about evangelical Christians, we need them now more than ever. Are evangelicals, as the ADL claims, really the greatest threat facing us Jews today? Last week, in northern Israel, IFCJ contributed $1-1/2 million for desperately needed fire trucks. The week before we brought 216 B'nei Menashe from India to Israel, and pledged millions of dollars in assistance to build shelters in Sderot near Gaza and throughout the northern Lebanese border, all with funds donated by Christians. Every year, these evangelical Christians contribute tens of millions of dollars through the Fellowship I head, helping 120 cities in Israel, over 200 projects, and countless countries in the former Soviet Union. Every day these Christians are feeding over 100,000 needy Jews around the world. Every day. Is it possible that these good people are really the greatest threat to Jewish life today? Moreover, they ask nothing in return, no *quid pro quo*, except that they be acknowledged, respected, and appreciated by the Jewish community and blessed by G-d.

But the organized Jewish community has utterly failed in reaching out to the evangelical community and joining in common cause with them on behalf of the survival of Israel and the Jewish people. I consider this a fault of catastrophic proportions, which is guided more by our own Jewish prejudices and stereotypes than by a sincere commitment to preserving Jewish lives.

What are my greatest concerns today with evangelicals?

Before he died, the former head of the ADL, Nate Perlmutter, shared with me his fear that the Jewish rejection of evangelicals could lead to a self-fulfilling prophecy, whereby such Christians would come to despise Jews for rejecting and constantly criticizing them despite their unconditional support. These good Christians would, in response to this constant rejection, become anti-Semitic, at which point the Jewish community would say, "see, we told you so." Thankfully, this has not transpired.

I have also been concerned that evangelicals may demand a *quid pro quo* on domestic policy issues in return for their support for Israel. Thankfully that, too, has not happened. Why? Because evangelical support is given out of unconditional love, out of a profound belief that G-d demands this of them, in order to bless the Jewish people.

I am concerned that despite the recent movement of some groups like AIPAC and even individual federations to cooperate with evangelicals, it is too little, too late, and frankly, too manipulative to be effective. It is wrong and myopic to use other people for our purposes instead of engaging in true dialogue and relationship-building with them. It was not an accident that I named the organization I founded some twenty-five years ago the International Fellowship of Christians and Jews, not the International Alliance of Christians and Jews.

I am also concerned that if Republican power wanes in Congress, Jewish interest in reaching out to evangelicals, a key component of that Republican power, will diminish with it. The fact is we need these people—for our very survival. There are parts of the world where Jews do not have great influence—for example South America, the Far East, and Australia, and even parts of the U.S. Why not turn to the millions of evangelical Christians in these areas to join us in standing for Israel? IFCJ has been investing millions of dollars in teaching and encouraging evangelical Christians to support Israel – in Canada, Europe, Latin America and the Far East, as well as here in the U.S., including among the Hispanic and African-American communities.

I should point out that this is not a call to change Christians' views and attitudes to be favorable toward Israel. Rather, I'm talking about inspiring, directing and channeling those feelings of support already present among evangelicals, in tangible meaningful ways through which they can demonstrate their love and solidarity with Israel. For thirty years the Jewish community has struggled to come up with a response to the challenge of how to relate to evangelicals and their support for Israel. Yet, incomprehensibly, this has never been a topic at the General Assembly of Jewish organizations. Even the National Jewish Community Relations Advisory Council (NJCRAC), already twenty years ago, issued calls to learn more about the evangelicals and engage them in dialogue and cooperation. To this day, that has not happened. Instead, most Jewish groups are stuck in their perception that "those people" are a threat to Jewish civil liberties and care more about ending abortions and homosexuality, and proselytizing Jews, than about Israel and the survival of the Jewish people.

What ought to be the Jewish response to evangelicals, especially if we believe as I do that today is 1938 all over again? There are those Jews, "Right wingers," who seek to use them to support Israeli settlements. And there are those on the Left who set up evangelicals as the bogeyman they must fight and defeat in the courts, lest they succeed in making America into a Christian nation and eroding Jewish civil liberties. The response that ought to guide our thinking, and that has guided me and the IFCJ for over thirty years, can be put pithily as follows: "cooperate whenever possible, oppose whenever necessary, and teach and sensitize at all times." To that end, our outreach to evangelicals should involve Jews of faith, not secular Jewish institutions, including all religious denominations—Reform, Conservative and Orthodox. For as Rabbi Abraham Joshua Heschel said, "faith must precede interfaith." Before closing, I want to urge that people read the recently published book *A Match Made in Heaven*, by Ze'ev Chafets, a Reform Jew who strongly advocates reaching out to evangelicals for the sake of Jewish survival. It is a must-read book.

My friends, it has been over thirty years since I initiated some of the first dialogues with evangelicals. In the course of those years I have often been attacked, even within my own Orthodox community. Yet we all have come a long way. As Senator Joe Lieberman recently said to me, "Yechiel, after 30 years you have finally been vindicated." Today, IFCJ has over 500,000 evangelical contributors who give close to $100 million annually to help Israel and Jews in need around the world. And more and more Jewish groups are finally realizing, albeit belatedly, that evangelicals are the greatest reservoir of (still essentially untapped) support for Israel and the survival of the Jewish people. It behooves us to at least meet them halfway.

Whether we like it or not, we Jews are part and parcel of the story of these Christians. But it is our choice whether and how we want to work with them so that hopefully they become friends, allies and partners, rather than—G-d forbid—the alternative, adversaries and enemies. We have enough of those already.

Today, Christians and Jews (and moderate Muslims) are in the same boat, fighting a battle against radical Islam. We ought to remember that on the missiles paraded down the streets of Teheran last year were the words "destroy the crusaders, kill the Jews." Whether we like it or not, we Jews and evangelical Christians are in the same boat. We had better wake up as a Jewish community and reach out in friendship to our friends. Because our very lives and the future the State of Israel and its citizens depend on it.

14

Social Justice and Jewish Survival

David Saperstein

First I am going to respond to some concerns raised by leading Jewish demographers about continuity. Two responses, in particular, are in order: first, if you care about the continuity of the Jewish people, consider what has been revealed by every major demographic poll in the Jewish community over the last thirty years about how Jews view their identity. By margins of two-to-one, even three-to-one, well *over* support for Israel or Jewish education or Jewish worship, individual Jews place committing to social justice, social ideals. It is far and away the most common expression of Jewish identity in America. In other words, when people are involved in the vast array of good deeds that they do, both Jewish and general, they believe they are playing out their Jewish values.

Now we may think that's good and we may think that's bad, but these results demonstrate that if we want to reach the Jewish community, we have to reach them where they are, and social justice is the most important gateway. If we can bring them back to deeper Jewish studying, Jewish spiritual meaning, Jewish ritual and Jewish communal rites through that kind of social idealism, it will be a success. But there is one thing I'm absolutely clear on: if the Judaism we offer our young people does not speak to the great moral issues of their lives, or the great moral issues of the world that they will inherit, it will not be one that will engage their hearts, their minds, or their loyalty.

Second, in speaking of the Religious Action Center and us, some have noted our "radical" position on Iraq. Is our view radical? I guess it depends on one's perspective. But, to be fair, did we call for immediate withdrawal? No. We called for a phased withdrawal and one that safeguards the security of our troops and the Iraqis, as well as stability wherever possible in the country. Did we call for a specific timetable? No. We did say we, though, that the administration ought to set some time table, because otherwise it simply wasn't going to withdraw. Did we call for a withdrawal of American troops from the region? No. We specifically said they should remain deployed in the region so that they could, if necessary, support Iraqi troops who will be fighting on behalf of the interests of the Iraqi government. They could maintain a presence in the Middle East to affirm other American interests in the region, including support for Israel.

We also affirmed our support for a whole series of steps we thought could be taken, based on what Republicans and Democrats are saying, which would have a better chance of politically stabilizing the situation. Engaging our friends and allies in the region, far more assertively, is an important way we can play a constructive role there. Whether we are right or wrong, these proposals are open for debate. A radical position? That seems a misleading statement of what the Reform Movement is, but let me clarify what the movement did do. It did say, above all, we want to have a debate in American Jewish life. What is happening in Iraq affects America, affects the lives our children will have, affects our ability to fight for freedom across the globe, affects our ability to fight the war on terrorism across the globe. One may think it is good for these purposes, one might think it is bad for them. But does anyone deny that it has a central impact on the essential Jewish concerns?

It has an enormous impact on Israel, for example. This war, whether we like it or not, has done more to strengthen Iran's hand in that region and to give it dominance there than anything that happened before. We may have gone into Afghanistan and eradicated the terrorist "class of 2001." But we went into Iraq and, through our mismanagement of the war, we have created the terrorist class of 2007. Those terrorists and insurgents have developed new techniques and new technologies for using terrorism against the world. These outcomes will plague Israel and the U.S. for generations to come.

So I don't know if we are right or wrong. What I know is that there ought to be a debate in our community on this issue, and that debate has not happened. Outside of our movement, when in the beginning of the war we were the only major national Jewish organization that came out publicly with the view that removing Saddam Hussein is a moral use of force, people said *shah*. "You shouldn't say that," they said, "people will think we're going to war because of Jewish interests in Israel." Later, when the war was so badly mishandled, we said there is no way to straighten this out militarily. So we have to try to find a combined military and political solution, and over a period of time militarily disengage from Iraq. And again, people said *shah*. Other than the Jewish Council on Public Affairs, I know of no national Jewish organization that has put the issue of Iraq on its national agenda, on the agenda of its national conventions or national board meetings, to talk about the issue and debate it. Come out with a position different from ours, let's have the debate.

When we went out to our community for two months we asked for a full-blown debate. We sent materials on all sides of the issues, equally, and there were debates that our synagogues held all over the country. We heard from people from every side of this issue. If anyone said let's be silent – because people may think we don't love the president who's good on Israel, or people may think that we are pushing war because we think it is good for Israel – if that mentality came from anywhere in the Jewish community, it was not from us. And I don't think Israeli or American interests are served by silencing that debate.

Now against that context let me turn to 1938. There is both good news and bad news about contrasting where we are religiously with 1938. For example, some good news: the long tradition of state-sponsored, church-sponsored, academic-sponsored anti-Semitism that was taught as part of the Christian world view, and that was so deleterious over the centuries, has clearly lessened here among all Christians, and among Evangelical as well as fundamentalist Christians. It's not that there are no problems. There are, but we don't have the ingrained kind of feeling of anti-Semitism that we felt earlier in this century.

It is commonly held that the Holocaust was rooted in Christian anti-Semitism. I want to submit something to think about: as intuitive as it may seem, there is actually comparably scarce historical evidence to substantiate this assertion. Christians believed in 1938 that they, too, might well be the victims. Few Nazi thinkers and leaders ever cited Christian texts or ideology as a justification for their views. Few Christian leaders, even those sympathetic to the Nazis, cited any connection between Christian anti-Jewish themes and Nazi anti-Semitism. And I can point to no historical record of Christian leaders who argue that the ideas that underlie Christian anti-Semitism justified the killing, the mass murder, extermination and genocide of the Jewish people. Nazi anti-Semitism was a radical break based on the pseudo-scientific racialism, this genetic idea of superior and inferior races, and of the mystical romantic nationalism that evolved in the mid-nineteenth century. It may well be, as I believe, that centuries of traditional Christian anti-Semitism created a fertile field in which Nazi anti-Semitism could flourish. But there is little historical evidence that Christian anti-Semitism led directly to Nazism or to the Holocaust.

It is against that background, then, that one can point to where Christians are today, particularly in the U.S. In contrast, I want to discuss where Muslims are. Although Jews were typically second-class citizens in Muslim countries, there was not the religious, academic, state-sponsored anti-Semitism that we found rooted in Christian ideology, culture, and politics. Recall many of the core ideas of Christian anti-Semitism: that of the "God- killer"; cessation of the Jewish covenant; blood libels; ritual murders. And then there was the transition into the Nazi ideas, portraying Jews as the greedy money lender, or the Protocols of the Elders of Zion, let alone the overt Nazi anti-Semitic imagery of Jews as germs in the body of humanity, as sub-human vermin whose total annihilation would be good for humanity. Those ideas, leading from Christian anti-Semitism and into Nazi anti-Semitism, apply virtually nowhere in Muslim history or in Muslim ideology. That is not to say there are no problems, not to say there aren't bad things in the Quran (there are bad things in the Bible too). But anti-Semitism was not seen as a normative tradition at any point in Muslim history. There were occasional waves of fundamentalism that wreaked havoc on the Jewish community, but the pattern of pogroms, of physical attacks on Jews, those were comparatively rare in Muslim history.

That is what makes this moment in Islamic history so alarming. It is alarming because almost out of nowhere, they have reached back, not into their own tradition, but into Christian anti-Semitic ideas and Nazi anti-Semitic ideas, and brought them into some of the extreme forms of Islam today. One is just as likely to hear citations to some of these Christian and Nazi ideas and see those images, such as the strong images on their web pages, as one is to see anything rooted in Islamic tradition. This is a trend that is truly frightening and cause for grave concerns.

So we talk about religion in 1938: as I said, there is good news and bad news. As regards the battle for Islam in the soul of Islam, there is a limit to what we can do. It will be won by Muslims. As Americans and as part of the worldwide Jewish community, we have to be sophisticated about how to help Muslim moderates who still, in numbers, predominate, though not in the voices that one hears. The irony is that often in the act of promoting moderates we actually legitimize their opponents, sometimes to the very people in the street whom we would like those moderate to be able to affect. So we have to be much more sophisticated about how we go about reaching the religious moderates in Islam, Hinduism, and other places across the globe where they predominate.

If we see an amelioration in some of the blatant anti-Semitism among the Evangelicals, it's not that I don't think there are real concerns we should continue to have. First, central to Evangelical theology is a belief that if they can bring good news to Jews they will do so. Appealing to us is part of their obligation, and that will be particularly relevant as we have assimilated kids—they are going to be targets of those efforts. More importantly on a political level, I am deeply concerned. For the politicized strands of fundamentalist Christianity pose serious dangers to America and the well-being of the Jewish community. They have taken efforts to gut the First Amendment, to tear down the wall separating church and state, to disadvantage the rights of women, gays and others, even some blatant efforts in some circles, albeit small ones, to Christianize America. These steps speak to a very different America than the one which has been so unique to the Jews, the one that honors the three Constitutional provisions: no religious tests for political office, no establishment of religion, and free exercise of religion. For the first time in human history, there was a country that said your rights and opportunities as a citizen would not depend upon your religious beliefs or your religious practices. What an extraordinary thing that has been for so many groups. Yes, like so many other rights promised at the point of our founding, it took generations to get there. But when we did, we enjoyed more freedoms, more rights, more opportunities in America then anywhere else in Jewish history. We should not walk away from that, even for the sake of making alliances with friends on behalf of Israel.

There are still some who are old enough to remember when there were quotas against Jews in major universities, when Jews were routinely locked out of country clubs, law firms and corporate board rooms. It is precisely during the period of the Warren and Burger Supreme Courts, specifically their assertions of the rights of women and minorities, blacks, Latinos, Jews, Catholics, disabled, agnostics, atheists, and others against the exclusive power of white male Protestants in this country, that we saw

Jews move from the peripheries of American society to the very center of political, professional, academic, and economic life. If the religious right succeeds in its efforts to reshape America and abandon the advances of the Warren and Burger courts, then our children and grandchildren will grow up in an America that is very different from the one that we have enjoyed.

What, then, of the cooperation between Evangelicals and Jewish communities on Israel? On the one hand, I agree that Israel needs all the friends it can get. And I recognize the power of the religious empathy toward Israel that emanates from the sincere belief that it is religiously compelled for America and Israel to be close. That Christian support provides a vitally needed sense of political, emotional and cultural energy in the pro-Israel community. I do not wish to engage the debate about whether or not they only care about Israel because of their pre-millennium ideas about Armageddon, but I think we can all agree that there are many who genuinely care about Israel for lots of reasons, including reasons we would and would not approve of. Pat Robertson, a few years ago, wrote in the Jewish web magazine *Olam* that Israel's 1967 conquest of Jerusalem opened up the last forty years of history, leading to an apocalypse that could culminate in atomic biological weapons, even a strike at the Earth from asteroids. And, he wrote, as the disaster approaches the Jewish people are going to begin to see their god, by which he clearly means Jesus in that context.

I once had a conversation with an Israeli prime minister about this, and he kind of jokingly said, "You know, David, either they're right or their wrong. If they're right, nothing we're gonna do is gonna make a difference anyway, and if they're wrong, let 'em do whatever they want to do, so long as they're supportive of Israel, right?" A good thought, and yet suppose they are using our influence with the White House to push policies that help bring this Armageddon, this millennial conflict between the forces of good and evil, closer. If they see American foreign policy through that filter, it is not going to be good for Israel, America, or the Jewish people. In addition, there are the Biblical literalists, who may support Israel for all kinds of reasons but who believe that the literal Bible has promised every inch of land to Jews and, therefore, are going use their political influence to do everything they can to oppose any effort in the peace process.

Now there may be some who think that's good, but I suspect many others are deeply troubled by that.

Who said these words here:

"I believe very strongly that we ought to support Israel; that it has a right to the land. This is the most important reason: Because God said so. In Genesis 13:14-17, the Bible says: The Lord said to Abram, 'Lift up now your eyes, and look from the place where you are northward, and southward, and eastward and westward: for all the land which you see, to you will I give it, and to your seed forever…Arise, walk through the land in the length of it and in the breadth of it; for I will give it to thee.' That is God talking. The Bible says that Abram…dwelt in the plain of Mamre, which is in Hebron, and built there an altar before the Lord. Hebron is in the West Bank. It is at this place where God appeared to Abram and said, "I am giving you this land," the West Bank. This is not a political battle at all. It is a contest over whether or not the word of God is true."

Those are the words of Senator James Inhofe of Oklahoma on the floor of the United States Senate, and if this is the approach that Evangelical Christians are going to bring, it is not good for Israel, not good for America, not good for the Jewish people. Again, I am not exaggerating that piece of it, but we should not ignore what it means, either.

Finally, there is the danger of making support for Israel a right-wing political phenomenon. We should be careful about that. On this, I think AIPAC has been fantastic, they have made the argument over and over again: what makes Israel unique is that it is non-partisan, it cuts across party lines, it cuts across ideological lines, and if one camp dominates over the other on the issue of the Jewish state, then Israel loses out. I think that this is true. So I'm willing to work with Evangelicals, but I will not buy their support by my silence or acquiescence on the vast part of their agenda that I think is harmful. They don't expect me to do it and I don't expect they will do that for me either.

So we work very closely with leaders on the religious right, on behalf of Israel and a whole range of other issues. And I think that that's good, because it helps the causes we are fighting for. I also think it is good because it is changing the face of the Evangelical community, opening it up, making it more tolerant and moderate and pluralistic, and I think it is good because it helps Israel. But it is particularly incumbent upon those of us who are willing to legitimize the folks on the religious right, and work with them in this area, that we stand up where we think they are wrong, and say it in the clearest possible terms, and fight for an America that will not only support Israel, but will continue to respect our most fundamental rights.

15

Europe's "Terrible Transformation?"

David Pryce-Jones

The old balance of power between the United States and the Soviet Union is no more, and tensions hitherto latent but contained have rushed into the global political vacuum. Muslims in particular, especially in the Middle East, experienced a freedom from foreign interference that they had not enjoyed for centuries. But freedom is one thing, consensus another. The relationship that Muslims will eventually reach among themselves—as Sunnis or Shiites, Islamists or nationalists, or anything else—is as indeterminate as ever. At the same time, the world of Islam has been in the process of deciding whether to accept Western modernity in whole, in part, or not at all.

Western Europe might well have been an uninvolved bystander to these dilemmas of other peoples' identity, except for the fact that since the 1950s and 1960s, Muslims have been immigrating in large numbers into all European countries. On account of incomplete census-taking and persistent illegal immigration, statistics are unreliable; but the figure of twenty million is widely accepted. European countries welcomed these newcomers, at first as workers, later as prospective citizens. Recently, under the banner of multiculturalism, they have been encouraged to build institutions to maintain their faith, their languages, and their customs.

Unconscious assumptions of superiority may well have misled Europeans into treating the phenomenon of Muslim immigration as purely a matter of economics. The advantages of living in Europe appeared so obvious that, it was expected, immigrants would naturally assimilate. Nobody of influence in public life paused to analyze what might be the social and political consequences of such a large-scale influx of people accustomed to defining themselves through a faith and a culture with a fierce history of war with Europe.

Organizations representing Muslim interests are now officially recognized in every European country. Also informing Islamic communal opinion and fortifying internal solidarity are mosques. In France there are 1,600 or so mosques, in Germany 2,200, and in Britain, according to one Islamic website, 1,689. Some of these organizations, and some imams of mosques, work for assimilation; others for separatism. In certain notorious cases, they seek to impose their faith and culture upon those of other faiths and cultures. Obeying a traditional concept of jihad—imperialism under an exotic cover—some Muslims have committed acts of terror, notably in Britain, France, Germany, and Spain, killing and wounding many (though fewer than were killed in America on 9/11). According to intelligence sources, over 1,000 potential jihad terrorists are under surveillance in Britain alone.

In several European countries, Muslim groups seek to influence and even to dictate foreign policy. Some also assert the right to determine what may be published about Islam itself, and demand the death penalty for those exercising free speech in ways they disapprove of. In 2005-6, cartoons of the prophet Muhammad, published in a Danish newspaper, were the pretext for demonstrations in one capital after another. In London, Muslims brandished placards inciting murder: "Behead those who insult Islam." In France, legal action was initiated (unsuccessfully) to stop reproduction of the cartoons. Following the lead of advocates like Tariq Ramadan in Switzerland or the extremist Abu Jahjah in Antwerp, some Islamic spokesmen have demanded the creation of a "sacred space" under which European Muslims will be ruled by shar'ia rather than the law of the land. Presumably this would protect, for instance, the many Muslims opposing the freedom of women, some of whom have been killed for choosing their own husbands or friends.

Ideas of this kind not only block assimilation but oblige non-Muslim majorities to consider at what point they will have to take measures in defense of their own identity. In the late 1930s, Winston Churchill had few supporters when he warned that appeasement of Nazism was a policy for which a very high price would have to be paid. What he called a "terrible transformation" was then taking place in the world. Obviously, Muslim extremism today lacks the leadership and the power of the Nazi state of the 1930s. But it already exhibits a dynamism, and a potential for mass mobilization, that bring within the realm of possibility another lasting transformation of Europe.

One determining factor here, about which much has been written, is that native Europeans have too low a birthrate to reproduce themselves.

Demographic extrapolations suggest that Muslims could become a majority in some places within the foreseeable future. The British towns of Bradford and Leicester, for instance, as well as the cities of Rotterdam in the Netherlands, Antwerp in Belgium, Marseilles in France, and Malmö in Sweden are among many in which an immigrant minority may soon outnumber the native population. Libyan president Muammar Qaddafi, articulating the hopes of numerous Muslim preachers and activists, has declared: "There are signs that Allah will grant Islam victory in Europe without swords, without guns, without conquests. The 50 million Muslims of Europe will turn it into a Muslim continent within a few decades."

In the face of facts like these, many European policy makers have taken refuge in appeasement, an option that postpones examination and hard choices. As one Swedish politician has put it, we must be nice to the Muslims while we are the majority, so that they will be nice to us when they are the majority. Being nice, indeed, has become the order of the day.

Thus, on the grounds that the Qur'an sanctions wife-beating, a German judge refuses to grant a divorce to a Muslim woman abused by her husband. British schools are advised not to teach the history of the Holocaust or the Crusades, for fear of offending Muslim children who will have learned at home that the former is an invention of the Jews to extract money and sympathy, and the latter a Christian crime. For the same reason, municipalities redesign Christmas celebrations to purge them of religious content. Hospitals remove crucifixes from their walls. Apologies are extended to Muslims who object vocally to the pope's theology, or to statues or artistic images deemed haram or forbidden, or to the design on ice cream said to look like the Arabic spelling of Allah, or to observances of Holocaust Memorial Day, or to innumerable other practices and details of life taken for granted by everyone else in the society.

Scattered across Europe today are perhaps over a million Jews, outnumbered by Muslims by a factor of twenty to one, probably more. Many Muslims, perhaps most, accept traditional stereotypes of Jews based on a few unquestioned verses in the Qur'an. Such customary prejudice is reinforced a hundredfold by the Arab and Muslim campaign against the state of Israel.

Indeed, the fate of the Jews of Europe has become linked to the fate of Israel in a way that virtually nobody seems to have anticipated. In 1996, the British historian Bernard Wasserstein published a book, *Vanishing Diaspora*, subtitled The Jews in Europe since 1945. It was a sober piece of work, but the perspective, however sorrowful, was essentially trouble-free. No danger was foreseen from the Right: Wasserstein quite correctly dismissed fascist relics of the past as having no general appeal. As a result of assimilation and intermarriage, Jews were destined simply to fade away in Europe until, he concluded, nothing would be left of them save "a disembodied memory." Muslims rated no more than two or three passing mentions in the book, and Islamism did not feature at all.

Today it remains true that, with minor exceptions, the principal threat to European Jews does not emanate from the Right. It emanates instead from a confluence of sources: a resurgent Islam, augmented powerfully by the culture of the European Left and the force of institutional opinion as embodied in the United Nations.

In theory, the UN ought to be the forum in which it would become established once and for all that Israel is a victim of aggression rather than the aggressor. In practice, the UN is the agency that more than any other works to enshrine the reversal of reality, and that has done so with increasing openness ever since the General Assembly's "Zionism is racism" resolution of 1975. Today, analogies between Israel and Nazism are as widespread as ever, if not more so, lately embellished by the charge that Israel practices a version of South African apartheid.

In one international forum after another, the Left has picked up and run with these vicious accusations, remodeling for contemporary purposes the anti-Jewish militancy of the Right in the 1930s. And not just of the Right. Indeed, the ideological pedigree of today's anti-Israel campaign in Europe can be traced less to Nazism or fascism than to the work of the Soviet propaganda machine that sprang into frenzied action after the Six-Day War of 1967. (Here, as so often, totalitarian systems become indistinguishable.) It is the Soviet-inspired condemnation of the United States and its allies, according to which the poor and oppressed everywhere are victims of American capitalism and culture, that the Left has perpetuated and revived time after time in the ensuing decades. By definition, then, Israel is in the wrong, and on two counts: as an ally of the United States, and as the alleged oppressor of Palestinians, a certified victim group of the third world.

Today's anti-Israel Left in Europe is a massed phalanx of German and Irish bishops, Anglican canons and Catholic priests, journalists from the leading papers of Europe, broadcasters (in particular at the BBC, which has gone so far as to suppress an in-house report of its bias against Israel), parliamentarians like George Galloway and Jenny Tonge, school and university teachers and trade unionists pressing for a boycott of Israel, and many others.

The Portuguese novelist José Saramago, winner of the Nobel Prize for literature, judged that a 2001 Israeli incursion into the West Bank city of Ramallah was "a crime that may be compared to Auschwitz." Gretta Duisenberg, wife of the Dutch former head of the European Central bank, sought a symbolic six million signatures for a petition to be presented at pro-Palestinian demonstrations in the Netherlands. Jan Guillou, president of the Swedish Association of Journalists, walked out of a meeting to commemorate the victims of 9/11 in protest that there was no mention of Muslims killed by Israel. According to the German socialist Oskar Lafontaine, "We must constantly ask ourselves through which eyes the Muslims see us." And so forth. Especially helpful to today's Left are Jews who themselves denigrate Zionism and the Jewish state. Such Jews, especially those with reputations in their professional fields, are featured prominently as signers of petitions and speakers at mass demonstrations where Palestinian and Hizballah flags are waving and the Israeli flag is likely to be burned.

As if all this were not alarming enough, the internal workings of the European Union have made things worse. At its core, the EU is bedeviled by a contradiction. If it is to survive and prosper and become the homogeneous international body it aspires to be, then its component nations must be reconceived as local regions or states in the American sense. By the law of unintended consequences, however, this homogenizing impulse has led to its opposite: namely, the reassertion of intense nationalist feeling among ethnic minorities long suppressed by the local majority. Basques, Burgundians, Bretons, Catalans, Corsicans, Welsh, Scots, Lombards, and others, their grievances nursed down the centuries, have all laid claim to their historic territories, and the EU has striven to accommodate these claims.

But that leaves Muslim immigrants and Jews as two minorities in Europe without a territory, pitted against each other by the EU in a competition for social space. Compounding the problem, the EU has chosen between them. The consistent condemnation of Israel by Brussels, alongside the EU's enormous and unaccountable subsidies to the Palestinian Arabs, has virtually institutionalized the polarization of these two landless communities.

Realizing too late the flaw in its doctrine, EU legislators have passed a range of laws designed to criminalize and punish both anti-Semitism and "Islamophobia." These laws are at best an expedient rather than a genuine remedy. For the most part, they have had the effect of choking off honest debate about the reality of the Muslim condition in Europe, and of encouraging Islamic extremists to take matters into their own hands and to cry "Islamophobia" when criticized. True, the EU has also set up a unit to monitor all aspects of racism; until recently, however, its reports were suppressed and re-edited to blur the fact that the high incidence of anti-Semitic behavior is closely tied to Muslims themselves. When Brussels does not wish to hear something, it simply closes its ears.

Countries define and report anti-Semitic incidents differently, so statistics are only suggestive. But, without doubt, they correlate with developments in the Middle East—and with the media's presentation of those developments. The latest, uncensored findings of the EU monitoring unit show that anti-Semitic incidents rose more or less steadily during Yasir Arafat's second intifada after September 2000. In 2002, for example, an Israeli raid on a terrorist base in the West Bank town of Jenin was reported almost universally as a war crime involving hundreds, even thousands, of innocent Palestinian victims. (In fact, in an area of about 100 square yards, fifty-two Palestinians had been killed, of whom thirty were in militia uniforms.) Anti-Israel outrage knew no bounds. All over Europe, attacks on Jews, synagogues, and other Jewish institutions followed.

According to the same source, anti-Semitic incidents over the period 2001-2005 increased in Germany from 1,424 to 1,682; in France from 219 to 504; and in Britain from 310 to 455, leaping to 594 in 2006. The incidents themselves, the EU report finds, have ranged from verbal aggression to physical assault, and most of the perpetrators have been Muslims. The report does not identify specific crimes. To take one example, though, in 2003 a young Algerian in Paris killed his Jewish neighbor, a disc jockey of about the same age. With hands still bloody from the deed, the assailant told his mother: "I killed my Jew, I will go to paradise." In January 2006, also in Paris, a mostly Muslim gang abducted the twenty-three-year-old Ilan Halimi, a sales assistant. When they failed to extort ransom, they tortured him, set him on fire, and left him to die.

The war with Hizballah in the summer of 2006 provoked another massive increase in anti-Semitic speech and deed. Some of the hostility was inspired by repeated denunciations of Israel's "disproportionate" defense of its citizens by European governments and media. Speaking for many, the Norwegian writer Jostein Gaarder, author of the international best-seller *Sophie's World*, wrote in August: "We no longer recognize the state of Israel…. To act as God's chosen people is not only stupid and arrogant, but a crime against humanity."

A well-researched report by the European Jewish Council has documented the anti-Semitism on display over the thirty-three days of last year's war. In Britain, for instance, there were an unprecedented 132 incidents. In France, there were sixty-one, as contrasted with thirty-four in the same period the previous year. A group in Germany counted more than 1,000 anti-Semitic acts in June and July (though most were related to Germany's hosting of the World Cup). While taking note of both neo-Nazi and extreme Left elements in the attacks, especially those in Central and Eastern Europe, the report concludes that primary responsibility rests with Europe's Muslim population. It might have added that the flames of anti-Semitism have been fanned by the universities, the media, and the EU itself.

This past March, the historian Benny Morris published an essay under the title, "The Second Holocaust Is Looming." Iran, Morris wrote, has clearly demonstrated its willingness to risk the future of the entire Middle East in exchange for Israel's destruction. One bright morning, not too long from now, the mullahs in Qom will meet in secret session under a portrait of the Ayatollah Khomeini and solemnly give the go-ahead to President Mahmoud Ahmadinejad, who has sworn to "wipe Israel off the map" and has been avidly pursuing the nuclear means of doing so. "With a country the size and shape of Israel," Morris concluded, "probably four or five hits will suffice: no more Israel."

Would anybody care? Morris's tone is one of almost elegiac resignation. Europeans, he writes, did little or nothing to save their Jewish fellow-citizens in the 1930s, and they would be no more willing to come to the rescue now. He might have added that in the past years they have busily been preparing the ground for their exculpation by insisting that Israel has brought it on itself.

A counterpart to Morris is the German writer Henryk Broder. In a recent book titled *Hurra, Wir Kapitulieren* ("Hurrah, We're Capitulating"), he charges that fear, cowardice, and concern for trade have combined to push Europeans beyond appeasement to the point of outright surrender to Islam. Each and every Islamist aggression is now answered by pathetic calls for "dialogue." Resistance is considered provocative, and a resort to force superfluous (if not illegal). As Islamization renders the continent progressively uninhabitable, illusion, denial, and defeatism reign supreme. In an interview, Broder advised young Europeans to leave while they can.

Whether one prefers Broder's sardonic scorn or the pessimism of Benny Morris, both of them, it may be, exaggerated for effect. Europe is now on the brink of another terrible transformation. Jews, whether Israelis or Europeans, are testing out the extent to which European civilization really has become hollowed out from within, and unable to withstand assault from without.

16

If Israel Ceased to Exist

Hillel Halkin

Can Israel, as the prime minister of Iran has bluntly put it, be wiped from the map? Of course it can be. The Iranian nuclear-weapons program has only added to the ways in which this can happen. Any small country whose larger neighbors, including those formally at peace with it, would be delighted, with the concurrence of a significant part of the human race, to see it vanish must reckon on its possible mortality. It has never been anything but foolish for Israelis, American Jews, or anyone else to deny this.

If Iran has made a difference, it is that an intermittent anxiety has now become a chronic one. In the past, acute concern over Israel's survival has arisen in times of war—1948, 1967, 1973—and abated once the military threat was over. But the Iranian threat is indeterminate. It has developed slowly and may be slow to go away, if ever it does.

And yet a successful Iranian nuclear attack, although it might effectively obliterate Israel in a matter of seconds, is not the most likely way in which Israel's destruction might take place. In fact, given Israel's technologically advanced anti-missile systems and its own nuclear deterrent, which could inflict calamitous retaliation, it is probably the least likely. Shiite eschatology notwithstanding, Iran's leaders would surely think more than twice before turning their own country into a giant suicide bomb. If Israel needs to fear nuclear suicide bombs, there is probably more to fear from terrorists who, surreptitiously supplied with them by Iran or others, might attempt to detonate several simultaneously, al-Qaeda-style, in Israel's major cities. Once initial radiation levels dropped, the numbers of dead, badly injured, and fatally or seriously ill, added to

127

the general havoc, might enable Arab armies to overrun a country too crippled to defend itself.

But Arab armies, should they at some not unimaginable future time attain conventional military superiority over Israel, could also destroy it without a single nuclear shot being fired. All they would need would be to possess, or to be allied with the possessor of, atomic weapons capable of neutralizing Israel's nuclear arsenal and preventing its deployment as a last-ditch measure were a conventional war about to be lost. Nor, once a beaten Israel surrendered, would widespread carnage have to be inflicted to finish the job. It would be enough for the occupying forces to encourage the "return" of millions of the descendants of the 1948 Palestinian refugees seeking to reclaim their families' properties. In such circumstances, Israel's conquered and demographically swamped Jews would wish only to flee. Presumably, the United States, the European Union, and other sympathetic countries would atone for the sins of the Holocaust by taking them in.

These are the envisionable cataclysms. But Israel's demise as a Jewish state could also take place less apocalyptically, by means of demographic swamping alone. There is a faster and a slower way for this to happen.

In the former, an Israel unable or unwilling to withdraw from all or most of the Palestinian West Bank would gradually turn into a bi-national state. Far from being a utopian solution to the Israeli-Palestinian problem, as it has been touted on the hallucinatory anti-Zionist Left, such a state, whose initial Jewish majority would be progressively eroded by a higher Arab birthrate, would be a dystopic horror. Everything we know about countries in which religiously and culturally heterogeneous populations with a long history of enmity are made to cohabit together without the clear dominance of one of them, or of a stronger third party, tells us that permanent and frequently violent conflict is the inevitable result. A bi-national Israel/Palestine would in all likelihood quickly degenerate into another Lebanon, with a demoralized and contracting population of Israeli Jews, steadily depleted by emigration, taking the place of Lebanese Christians.

This is the worst-case demographic scenario. But even if Israel withdraws to, or nearly to, its 1967 borders, with or without a peace settlement with the Palestinians, its demographic future will be precarious. In the absence of large-scale Jewish immigration, and even assuming a steady drop in Israeli-Arab birthrates as the Arab standard of living rises, Israel's Jewish majority, whose ratio to its Arab minority was 10-to-1 in the 1950s and now stands at 4-to-1, will continue to shrink, almost certainly to 3-to-1 and possibly well beyond that before some sort of stasis is achieved.

The greater this shrinkage, the more Arab-Jewish tensions will grow, with Arab demands to do away with Israel's expressly Jewish character becoming more clamorous. At some point the situation could spiral out of control, again leading to endemic violence accompanied by Jewish emigration and irredentist calls for the anschluss of heavily Arab areas (like the Galilee) to a Palestinian state next-door. Even without the intervention of Arab armies from neighboring countries, such an Israel, too, could end in dismemberment. Just as the enemies of Zionism predicted, Israel would have turned out to be a foreign beachhead in the Middle East that could not hold out forever against the sheer weight of the Arab multitudes ranged against it.

Not even peace with the Palestinians and the Arab world, then, will necessarily ensure Israel's long-term survival. Nor, as desirable as it is for Israel to treat its Arab citizens equally, is there any reason to believe that, thus treated, they would accept living in a Jewish state once a demographic tipping point were reached. As long as Palestinian and Arab nationalism and Islamic religious militancy persist, Israel will never be like Belgium, in which roughly equal numbers of Walloons and Flemings co-exist peacefully despite ethnic tensions between them—and Belgium, too, may one day break apart. Israel's only hope is to stay clear of the tipping point.

And yet here we encounter a curious fact. The same American Jewish community that is so worried about Israel's survival has consistently failed to do the one thing in its power that could have most helped to assure it.

The statistics speak for themselves. In 2005, for example, 3,005 Jews from France, a country with a Jewish population of a half-million, immigrated to Israel; the United States and Canada combined, with roughly twelve times as many Jews, provided 2,987 immigrants. And should it be objected that this comparison is unfair, inasmuch as French Jews have had to live in recent years with a degree of anti-Semitism unknown in America, the objection is borne out only slightly. In the sixty years of its existence, during most of which anti-Semitism was no problem for the Jews of France, Israel was chosen by 75,000 of them. The figure for North American Jews for the same period is 118,000, seven times smaller proportionally—or approximately one Jew in 3,000 per annum.

What would have happened had American Jewish immigration to Israel since 1948 been proportional to that from France, which has not been dramatically high itself? Nearly a million more American Jews would have gone to live in Israel. Had this happened, Israel's Jewish population would be six-and-a-half million today. The Jewish-Arab ratio would be 5-to-1 rather than 4-to-1. The tipping point would be significantly farther away, and the prospect of still more American Jewish immigrants in the future might have put an Israel within sensible borders out of the demographic danger zone.

The effect on Israel of negligible American Jewish immigration has been more than merely demographic. It has been more than merely socio-cultural and socio-economic, too, though one cannot but think wistfully of the contribution that a million more American Jews, with their education, talents, values, and dynamism, might have made to Israeli life. It has also been psychological. It has been part of the way in which Israel and American Jewry, although they have been obvious sources of strength to each other, have also been great mutual disappointments. These disappointments go to the core; they strike at the heart of Jewish identity.

Historically, few things have been more basic to this identity than the great narrative of exile and return that is a leitmotif of Judaism, the story of a people, like none other, repeatedly driven from its land and repeatedly dreaming of regaining it, since there alone could it be its true self. Well before the advent of political Zionism, it is true, there were Jewish thinkers who suspected that the true Jewish self was the false self, so to speak, of the Diaspora. Already in the twelfth century we find Yehuda Halevi writing scathingly in his philosophical polemic, the *Book of the Kuzari*:

> All our prayers [to return to Jerusalem and the land of Israel],
> such as "Let us bow to His sacred mount" and "He who restoreth
> His presence to Zion" and the like, are merely the prattle of par-
> rots and the caw of starlings, since we do not mean what we say.

Yet not even Halevi was ever shaken in his conviction that the inner striving of Jewish history was homeward. And while even after the inception of the Zionist movement in the late nineteenth century the number of Jews actively seeking to settle in Palestine comprised, prior to the rise of Nazism, a small minority of Diaspora Jews, Zionism could justly claim that it was a revolutionary movement in Jewish life, and that all revolutions, however genuine the aspirations they represent, begin with small, dedicated cadres. These succeed because their founders correctly assess the popular support for them that can be mobilized even if it does not originally exist.

Still, the fact remains that, even after the establishment of a Jewish state, the overwhelming majority of Diaspora Jews have chosen, in the absence of internal pressures to emigrate, to remain where they are—and nowhere more so than in the United States. Considering that there has never been in the Diaspora a better place than the United States for Jews to live, this may be no cause for surprise. Surprising or not, however, 99 percent of American Jews have not thought, and do not think today, that the benefits of living in a sovereign Jewish state outweigh the advantages of life in America.

This has delivered a message, however surreptitious, to Israelis. As much as we American Jews are prepared to exert ourselves on Israel's behalf, it has said to them, there is a limit beyond which we will not go. The Jewish narrative of exile and return is a heroic myth; in practice, however, our ordinary lives are good enough for us. Indeed, if we were honest with you we would admit that, while we sometimes complain about Israeli cynicism, no one has done more to make you cynical than we have. Zionism told you that you were the vanguard of a people, and that if you went first and made a home for it, the people would follow. But Zionism lied to you, because we never intended to follow. And since we can read the figures as well as you can, and understand that it would be in our vital interest to reinforce you if we believed that our survival depended on yours, you are right to conclude that we do not believe it. If Israel goes under, we will grieve and get over it, just as Jews have gotten over their grief so many times before in their history.

This statement has been made, as it were, sotto voce. It has not been meant for the ears of American Jews themselves, let alone for those of Israelis. But Israelis have heard it loud and clear. More than that: they have been convinced by it. Not only did they long ago cease to hope that American Jews might join them, they long ago ceased criticizing their fellow countrymen for joining American Jews. There are today an estimated half-million Israelis living in the United States, many times the number of American Jewish immigrants in Israel. And why shouldn't there be? If America is the best place for an American Jew to live, why isn't it the best place for an Israeli Jew? And if Jewish life in America will survive Israel's destruction, why shouldn't a prudent Israeli seek a safe haven there now? American Jews should be the last to complain when Israelis forsake Israel for America. It is they who have issued the invitation.

But the disappointment cuts both ways. If the Jews of Israel feel let down, so do American Jews, including many who count themselves among its supporters.

Israel is not the Jewish state these American Jews hoped for. Interminably at war with its neighbors, ridden by internal tensions and political corruption, lacking leaders of stature, out of favor with enlightened opinion everywhere, its people fearful for the future, not only is such a country not, as David Ben-Gurion proclaimed it would be in 1948, a light unto the nations, it is not even a light unto the Jews.

If the Jews of America were like other hyphenated Americans, this might be of little consequence. But the Jews of America are different. Not only are many of them more emotionally involved with Israel than other Americans are with other countries; and not only are they therefore more identified with Israel by other Americans than other Americans are with other countries; they also have a different image of themselves than do other Americans from other countries—and Israel, in recent years, has given this image a beating. It has delivered to the Jews of America a message of its own. It goes like this:

Although we may prefer not to acknowledge it in the presence of Gentiles, we Jews, whether because we have prided ourselves on being chosen by God or on having chosen Him, have always considered ourselves to be more advanced, more rational, and more morally refined than others. Throughout our worst periods in the Diaspora, we have comforted ourselves with the thought that the world's rejection of us was proof, not of our faults, but of its foolishness, the same foolishness that caused it to create the cruel and unjust societies we were forced to inhabit. This is what happens, we told ourselves, when Gentiles run the world. How much better a place it would be if Jews could run it. How much better a place it would be in religious or secular messianic times, when it was run by Jewish principles!

And yet, so this message continues, we have for the past sixty years run a tiny part of the world, and look what we have made of it. Although we may produce more than our share of Nobel Prize winners and hi-tech wizards, when given the full responsibility for managing our own affairs that we never had in the Diaspora, we have shown ourselves to be no more competent than the Gentiles. Clearly, we have deceived ourselves, our belief in Jewish superiority having been possible only so long as others were in charge. While we thought of exile as a misfortune, it alone enabled us to nurture grandiose notions about ourselves that had no basis in reality.

It can be cogently argued, I believe, that on both a conscious and an unconscious level, the fear of losing the sense of Jewish specialness explains a great deal of Jewish anti-Zionism, that of the "progressive" Jewish Left no less than that of the "reactionary" ultra-Orthodox Jewish Right. Behind their principled affirmation of the Diaspora, whether as a human opportunity to interact with the world and improve it or as a God-imposed chastisement that must be borne patiently, has lain the understanding that Jews in a Jewish state must of necessity become many things that in the Diaspora were left to the Gentile: strutting generals, crooked politicians, mindless bureaucrats, hypocritical diplomats, flag-waving jingoists, provincial intellectuals, parasitic clergymen, bribable policemen, brawling football fans, and above all, millions of ordinary people who stopped dreaming Jewish dreams because they were living the plebeian fulfillment of one of the greatest of them.

If, then, despite all that American Jews have done for Israel, they have not done what Israel needed most, the reverse is equally true. In fighting Jewish assimilation in America, after all, Israel can offer only limited practical aid. Evenings of Israeli folk dancing and Israel Independence Day parades will not prevent millions of American Jews from marrying out or losing their Jewish identity; neither will bringing them by the chartered planeload to tour Israel, no matter how reassuring its normality may seem to them. On the contrary: the only Israel that could change the self-image of the marginal American Jew would be one that gave him a sense of Jewish uniqueness. In the years immediately following its brilliant victory of 1967, this was indeed what Israel did; the luster of those years, however, wore off long ago.

Today, if Israel has any effect on marginal Jews in America, it is more likely a negative one. Universalist in outlook, liberal in politics, such Jews ask themselves: if this is who the Jewish people turn out to be when left to their own devices, why be part of them? And why cause myself, by living as a Jew, to be associated by other Americans with a country that—at least in the circles I move in—is not esteemed, even if it has not yet become, as it now is in Europe, one of the most certifiably disliked places on earth?

Israel, contrary to conventional wisdom in the organized American Jewish community, may today be more of a spur to assimilation than a bulwark against it. One thinks of the Roman Empire after the bloody suppression of the two great Jewish revolts against Rome in the years 67 and 132 C.E. Although this is not stressed in internal Jewish sources, it is a commonplace for historians today to observe that many people in this period left Judaism for Christianity, or chose Christianity over Judaism, because of the stigma of being associated with a failed and unpopular Jewish nationalism. It may well be that historians of the future will say something similar about Jewish life in our own times.

Of course, deeply religious Jews, who have a transcendent rationale for being Jewish, will not be influenced by such considerations. Such Jews will go on existing in the United States with or without Israel; let it be destroyed and—global weather permitting—they will still be praying and studying a thousand years from now. Although assimilation and intermarriage will run their course, and the descendants of most American Jews alive today will disappear from the ranks of the Jewish people, the numbers of ritually observant Jews, for whom alone procreation continues to be a prime commandment of Judaism, will continue to grow.

Should Israel vanish, I myself would not find the existence of such an American Jewry to be of any interest. Seen from the perspective of a non-observant Jew, a thousand more years of synagogue-going do not strike one as a fit continuation of the great historical adventure that being Jewish has been until now. And while Judaism in the Diaspora would continue to evolve in the future as it has done in the past, the Jewish people has been there before, too. Coming after the immense and open-ended Jewish drama of Israel, such questions as whether American Jewish women should be called to the Torah, or American Jewish homosexuals should be allowed to become rabbis, strike me as trivial.

But even from within, from the perspective of Jewish observance, would there not be something dishearteningly pointless in life after the death of Israel? After all, what is it that Judaism has been telling the world ever since it and Christianity parted ways? Is it not that, unlike Christianity, it is not just a faith but a way of life that seeks to permeate every aspect of existence, and that it can therefore only demonstrate its true worth when every aspect of existence is permeated by it? What then, if not a Jewish state, in which alone such permeability exists, can be Judaism's ultimate test? And what would be the purpose of a religious existence that, without having finished taking this test, its first attempts at which did not earn it high marks, was reduced to facing lesser challenges again? Would it not be a stale anti-climax even to itself.

It is possible to think of Israel as the psychiatrist's couch on which the Jewish people has lain down after long centuries of Diaspora life. Israel forces Jews to surrender fantasies and illusions about themselves that have long been part of their character. It has, literally and figuratively, brought the Jewish people down to earth. As is always the case with punctured ego ideals, this is painful. Still, it is liberating to know who you are, however belatedly, even if it is not who you thought you were.

Except that, at precisely this point, the world has chosen to think otherwise. At the very historical moment when Israel has obliged Jews to come to terms with their ordinary humanity, Israel has more and more impressed ordinary humanity in the opposite manner. Not only has it failed to gain acceptance by a good part of the world as an ordinary country, it has aroused reactions and emotions that ordinary countries do not arouse. The world declines to see it in ordinary terms.

This is increasingly true of Israel's friends no less than of its enemies. Israel's strongest non-Jewish supporters, especially in America, are now evangelical Christians. Certainly, the discomfort many Jews feel with the backing of evangelicals owes much to the latter's conservative political agenda; certainly, too, it stirs visceral Jewish fears of Christian religious fervor, which has rarely redounded to the benefit of Jews. But it is also related to the larger-than-life role in which evangelicals have cast the Jewish people and Israel, a role in which, regardless of whether a Christian or a Jewish script is written for it, secular Jews, in Israel and the Diaspora alike, are increasingly unable to recognize themselves.

Yet Christian philo-Semitism, however it may exaggerate Jewish virtues and induce fears of what may happen if its high image of the Jews ever collapses, is hardly the greatest problem facing them. This distinction continues to be reserved for anti-Semitism, and especially for that variety of it that manifests itself as an extreme hostility toward the state of Israel. And because anti-Israelism is now badly infected by anti-Semitism, it too attributes qualities to Israel and the Jews that do not belong to ordinary human life. Israel is not just one of many countries ruling another people that wishes to be free of it, it is a reincarnation of Nazism; it is not another nation-state stubbornly trying to make a go of it in an ostensibly post-national age, but the very avatar of reactionary tribalism in a new era of global brotherhood; its Jewish supporters are not merely a well-organized political force, they secretly run the world's most powerful country from their hidden seats of power, and so on and so forth.

In the face of such charges, many Jews feel a mental helplessness greater than in the past because their sense of themselves is more diminished than in the past. Once, when they believed more in their own exceptionalism, it was possible for them to understand anti-Semitism as the hateful distortion of that belief, its sinister mirror image in which all the good in them was reversed. Did the anti-Semites accuse them of being an infernally arrogant people who refused to mix with the rest of the human race? Yes, they did refuse, but their mission was not infernal but divine. Were they blamed for thinking they were better than others? Of course they thought that—because they were. Was their invisible hand at the center of everything? No, but everything indeed revolved around them, for they were the indispensable ingredient, the magical leaven, that would uplift the entire human race.

Today Jews are left staring at the distorted mirror image alone. The figure that stood before the mirror is gone.

The world, then, miscasts the Jews. It has not yet realized that they are not as different or as important as it thinks they are.

Or is it possible that, however distorted its image of them may be, it knows something about them that they no longer do?

This is a question to be asked with trepidation. There is good reason for a religiously skeptical Jew to be dismayed by the thought that his people are forever destined or doomed to a special and inescapable fate. Before picking up the gauntlet that is again being flung at their feet, Jews should be wary of slipping back into the delusions that Israel should have cured them of.

I have in mind those conceptions that would again place Israel and the Jewish Diaspora, linked in common cause and purpose, at the epicenter of history by means of some new, secularized version of Jewish specialness: Israel and the Jews as the front line of democracy, Israel and the Jews as the standard bearers of Western civilization, Israel and the Jews as the world's shock troops against Islamofascism, Israel and the Jews as the canaries in the coal mines of the new barbarism, etc., etc.—anything, in a word, but Israel and the Jews as a small country and nation that have carried the burden of specialness long enough and paid too heavy a price for it.

This is not to say that all of these things may not, in some sense, be true. It is simply to observe that Jews should not hurry to embrace them without an awareness of the inner need they serve, the need to recover that belief in their own uniqueness, as a people chosen by history if not by God, that they have lost but still crave.

Do Jews really want to be at the epicenter? Is this a role they are prepared to play? Is it one they are capable of playing? Can enough of them even agree on what this role is? And again: do they have any choice about it? If this is where the world has put them, what difference do their own desires make?

The Jews are a conundrum. When all is said and done—and what hasn't been said about them and what hasn't been done, to them and by them?—there is something inexplicable about the monumental place assigned to them, by themselves and by others, over the centuries. Israel and America, each in its way, has demystified them; must they now be re-mystified? If the burden of Jewish history is to be shouldered by them once more, should they at least not know clearly what it consists of?

If Iran goes nuclear, the possibility of Israel's destruction becomes greater. But the possibility is there without Iran, too. How important is it to prevent it? And how important to whom?

We are not necessarily, as has been suggested, on the brink of catastrophe, as in the years leading up to World War II. Indeed, things haven't been this good for the world's Jews in 2,000 years. Nearly half of them are concentrated in an independent Jewish state, wealthier and more powerful than any that existed in antiquity. Most of the other half live in stable democracies in which they are economically well-off and safe from all serious harm.

In only one respect are things worse. In the 1930s the Jews were a people that had lost a first temple and a second one; yet as frightful as their next set of losses was to be, they did not have a third temple to risk. Today, they do. And in Jewish history, three strikes and you're out.

17

Challenges and Dangers Facing American Jewry

David Harris

Let me begin with a story. Before the tunnel was built between England and France there was a tender offer, and under the rules of the British government it was required that the lowest bid be considered first. And among all the bids that came in for building this massive engineering feat to link Britain with the continent, costing in the billions of pounds, there was one that came in at 10,000 British pounds. And it came from a previously unknown construction firm named Goldberg and Shapiro. The British government was puzzled at having never heard of this firm, but it was obligated under law to go and meet with the principals, and they did.

They found themselves in the east end of London in a poor neighborhood. And they saw the name of the firm on the outside of a ramshackle building. They walked up to the third floor and they knocked on the door. An elderly gentlemen answered and they said, is this Goldberg and Shapiro? "Yes it is, I'm Goldberg," he said. "Well, we are here from the British government to understand how you intend to build this tunnel linking Britain and the continent for 10,000 pounds." And he said, "well in actuality it is very simple. You see I go to Dover and my partner Shapiro goes to Calais. Each of us has a shovel, we raise the shovel and wave at each other and we start digging toward each other and voila! We meet mid-way and you have your tunnel." It took a few moments for the British to digest this before asking, "What happens if the two tunnels don't meet?"

To which Mr. Goldberg replied, "in that case you get two tunnels for the price of one. "

Why do I offer this story? First, for a moment of levity. But I also mention this tunnel story for a different reason. I am a political activist. My approach to things is slightly different. I look at the day-to-day, and for me the most important element in the day-to-day of my work is insuring that there is a tunnel, or if you will, a bridge, that firmly links the U.S. and Israel, and that an essential lane, if not lanes, within that tunnel are occupied by American Jews and Israeli Jews, come what may.

After three decades in this business, I have come to what should be a very obvious conclusion: there essentially is no substitute for the U.S.-Israeli bilateral relationship, especially in the life of Israel. If the U.S. were somehow to reconsider its strategic position, if it were to distance itself from Israel, redefine its special relationship with the Jewish state, what would happen? In my assessment a great deal would happen. A great deal would happen because nothing can replace, in the life of Israel, the role played by the U.S. in virtually every sphere of Israeli policy, military, strategic, defense, economic, diplomatic, political and civil life. And I also believe that while American Jewry has not been the sole ingredient in explaining that special relationship, it most certainly has been a key ingredient. And I also know that until 1967, it was not the U.S. that played that role in Israel's life as a friend. And we as Americans and American Jews and friends of Israel need to understand that countries can reassess their own geopolitical and geo-strategic perspectives.

I'm not a lawyer, but to the best of my knowledge there is nothing in the U.S. Constitution that says the U.S.-Israel special relationship is set in stone for all times. Israel would have had a much more difficult time in the 1967 war had it not been for French-built and French-provided weaponry, and particularly Mirage aircraft. And yet by the mid-1960s, in the wake of Algerian independence, France was reassessing its geo-strategic interest and we all know what happened. As a consequence it seems to me that our role in Israel's life on a day-to-day basis remains absolutely essential unless we are prepared to see one day a wedge driven between Israel and the U.S.

Believe me, there are those in this country who would like to see that wedge driven between our two nations, and who are trying to forge the kinds of alliances that will one day neutralize, perhaps, the impact of the pro-Israel community in this country. We cannot afford to let that happen, not simply because of that bilateral role I described, but also because once the U.S. begins to remove itself, that development will serve as a disincentive to peace in the region. If Arab countries believe that over time a gap will grow between America and Israel, and that American Jewry will become less and less of a factor, increasingly unconcerned with what happens in Israel, then this may indeed whet the appetites of those who have long thought to reorient American foreign policy in the first place. For similar reasons it will also provide, as I said, a disincentive for peace.

Secondly, from my perspective—and far be it for me, living here, to suggest how Israel should conduct its internal affairs—from here in the U.S., Israel is still a work in progress and we ought not to be too harsh in our judgment of a nation that is fifty-nine years young and still new to the practice of statecraft. All the more so when in reality we have a unique nation, which is trying to juggle, on the one hand, the often-amoral requirements of diplomacy and international politics, and on the other hand, trying to adhere, however it may define itself, to a certain ethical code, not of a nation but of a people. How do you juggle these two elements of sovereignty and peoplehood in a state? And I would suggest that if we went back in history to 1776 plus fifty-nine, we would be rather harsh, I suspect, in our judgment of where our country was on foundational questions, even against the standard provided by the promise of our founding document. This is not to say that, therefore, *ipso facto*, Israel will over time necessarily resolve the messy issues it faces and that we all-too-often witness ourselves in our daily reading of the press. For Israel is also uniquely juggling its experiment in sovereignty and its experiment in the symbiosis between what we euphemistically call a Jewish and a democratic state. It is doing this without even being able to define precisely, in consensual form, what it means to be a Jewish state, or how to balance the Jewish elements with the democratic elements—all the more so when they come in conflict, as they can. Again, I think we need a certain measure of patience, though always mixed with perseverance.

And this brings me to the third point. There is an area where American Jews actually do have certain unique interests in how Israel's soul will be defined in the years ahead. A week ago today, we marked *Yom HaShoah*, Holocaust Remembrance Day. Some of us were quite struck by the comments of a former Israeli chief rabbi, who used the occasion to blame the *Shoah* on Reform Judaism. Now we mark *Yom Hazikaron* running into *Yom Ha'atzma'ut*, as we know: Israel's Memorial Day running into Independence Day. And yet, just days ago in Israel there was a local council that refused an Israeli Reform rabbi's request to chant the funeral incantation of *Eil Molai Rahamim*, having lost his son in the Lebanon war. He was rejected, we are told, because others in the council refused a liberal rabbi's right—irrespective of whether he lost his son or not—to chant the prayer. We have a stake in the outcome of these debates.

People like myself and my organization, the American Jewish Committee, are loath to get involved and take steps ahead of any Israeli government that is trying to address issues of war and peace and national security. In our view, that would be the ultimate *chutzpa*. Still, on Jewish identity issues and related internal matters, we do have a role to play, because ultimately the Israel that emerges from this struggle that goes on, and has gone on perhaps eternally, will help determine whether we can identify with that Israel or not.

This brings me finally to the theme of 1938. As worrisome as the times are, as dangerous as the times are, it is not 1938 again. In 1938 we had the year of the German imperial *Anschluss*. That was the year of the creation of Flossenberg and Mauthausen. It was the year of the appeasement leading to the ill-fated Munich conference and the sacrifice of Czechoslovakia on the altar of political expediency. The year 1938 was when the Nuremberg laws were extended to Austria; 1938 was the year that Italy introduced its first anti-Semitic laws. And 1938 was the year that Waffen SS was created. We have enough challenges today without conjuring up those images that only lend themselves to hyperbole and panic.

At the same time, I share the worry of others about the demonic quality of what has become anti-Israel criticism. And again, as a political activist I need only point to the U.N. Human Rights Council in Geneva, the body that was created last June to replace the dysfunctional, discredited Human Rights Commission. I would urge people to look for themselves at its record during its first nine months, but I'll give a hint: nine resolutions that have criticized one country and one country alone, Israel; one weak, flabby attempt to address the genocide in Darfur, but the member states could not even bring themselves to criticize Sudan. How can one discuss Darfur without discussing Sudan's role? And I also would agree that Israel's predicament in the messy world in which it operates, in which all countries operate, ought not to be used as an excuse or pretext for illegitimate behavior.

Finally, I believe that there is a great responsibility that some Israeli observers have properly placed on our shoulders as American Jews. The detachment of American Jews from Israel in too many cases is new. It is not entirely the fault of Israel, however graciously some of them would like to present things. It is our own fault. We must bear the responsibility, as well, for the growing indifference. Is it necessarily spurring assimilation? No. At the same time, however, we do need to introduce Israel into our lives far more than we have – Israel as it is, and not only Israel as we would idealize it to be. Too often we American Jews have spent too much time romanticizing the Israel of our fertile imagination, only to generate the predictable disappointment among ourselves, and especially future generations, when the Israel of today's reality falls far short of the Israel that we have conjured up in our minds.

18

Dilemmas of Jewish Survival as Seen through the Prism of Shakespeare's *The Merchant of Venice*

Susannah Heschel

During the first years of its staging, Shakespeare's play, *The Merchant of Venice*, which was identified as a comedy, evoked uproarious laughter in the audience during Shylock's famous speech, "Hath not a Jew eyes." How absurd, audiences seem to have thought, that Shylock would imagine that the body of a Jew and that of a Christian would have anything in common! How typical of a Jew to speak of the physical body and not, like a Christian, speak in elevated terms of the supreme significance of the soul. By the eighteenth century, however, Shylock was portrayed not for laughs but as diabolical and vengeful. No longer merely comical, his speech was seen as a foretaste of an insidious demonic plan to murder the Christian Antonio, symbolic, in Christian imagination, of the demonic wish of Jews to destroy all Christians. That changed in the nineteenth century, when Shylock became a tragic figure who evoked silence or even sympathy. Actors started portraying Shylock as a persecuted Jew, symbolic of centuries of Christian intolerance. Audiences felt sympathy for him, as illustrated in the highly popular 1817 Victorian novel, *Harrington*, by Maria Edgeworth, which used Shylock as part of the Bildungsroman of a young, wealthy London man trying to overcome his anti-Semitism.

Finally, when *The Merchant of Venice* appeared on the Yiddish stage in the early twentieth century, Shylock became a figure of dignified pathos and audiences were brought to tears in their identification with him. He was the victim of Christian anti-Semitic abuse, not the antagonist of Antonio, and yet he was able to rise above the abuse in his extraordinary dignity and, especially, his refusal (as the Yiddish script rewrote the courtroom scene) to take his pound of flesh: Jews don't kill, cried out the famed Yiddish actor Maurice Schwartz in the 1948 production, as he threw down his knife.

By contrast, in the state of Israel, as Avraham Oz has pointed out, The Merchant of Venice has virtually always been a critical failure—and in that we see a signal of Zionism's great success. Israelis lack the context of the Diaspora mentality of persecution and affliction to find the play compelling, and they have little interest in the nuances of Christian theological anti-Judaism—poles of mercy and vengeance—that are reflected in the play. That absence of Jews being culturally shaped—or disfigured —by the Christian anti-Semitic context is part of the glory of Zionism: to have created a cultural realm in which the pathologies of the master narrative of the Christian West are simply irrelevant. And yet at the same time, this is one of the dangers: namely, the naïveté of Israeli culture regarding Christianity and the anti-Semitism of the Diaspora, its pervasiveness, subtlety, and power. That, in turn, is combined in problematic ways with classical Zionism's repudiation of the Diaspora to create Israeli Jews who, as Jeffrey Goldberg recently pointed out, have repudiated Jewishness. Describing young Israelis in army service, Goldberg writes that they have become "indifferent to the idea that Israel was meant to serve some sort of cosmic purpose, either a universal purpose, as a light unto the nations, or a tribal purpose, as an ark of refuge for lost and suffering Jews.... As for Western Jews, those few still clinging to the fantasy of physical and spiritual redemption, they were pitied."

As others have noted, Israel stands before us in a crisis of identity, reflected in a sense of loss of purpose as well as heritage, a crisis felt strongly by many Israelis. The crisis has even led a few Israelis to a repudiation of the Jewish state and an alliance with those outside Israel who advocate academic boycotts and economic divestiture. Such developments are not only the result of a failure to understand the Jewish identity at the heart of Israel and Zionism, but also the consequence of the afflictions of war, terrorism, and violence, corruption within the government and business sectors, and omnipresent militarization of Israeli society, to say nothing of the forty-year occupation. And yet it is precisely on this point that American Jews might have something to offer.

Neither Israeli nor Jewish identity can be forged in a vacuum. We exist as Israelis and Jews in Statehood and in Diaspora not only as we conceive ourselves, but as objects of mythic invention by the rest of the world. Why is Israel constantly raked over the coals, examined in such minute detail in our newspapers? Why has Israel become such an overdetermined symbolic template for moral condemnation? "The world has miscast us," Goldberg writes, by placing us "at the epicenter of history" and we have embraced that position with our "belief in our own uniqueness," a sense of "Jewish grandiosity." What Israel has taught us, he writes, is "that we Jews are more ordinary than we have imagined." Zionism longs for normalcy, for Israel to be like all the nations, but its politics are too often rooted in claims to inimitability that have indeed marked Jewish history, from the very fact of our survival since antiquity, our existence as a "state of exception" in the societies of Christians and Muslims through the centuries, and our destruction in the historically unique event of the Shoah, the Holocaust.

Our identity is not rooted in reality alone, nor can the Jewish people by ourselves overcome the magical roots of the world's view of us. As a state, Israel may try to make us ordinary but we are still mythic figures, Shylocks, in the minds of the Gentiles, and in subtle, often unconscious ways, we collectively enact Shylock by appealing to the world's fears of us as well as its pity for us. How do we uproot those myths when they are rooted in magical thinking masquerading as theology and morality in the discourse of Christians and Muslims? Here is one example that undergirds Christian hostility toward Zionism: the gospels tell the story of a non-Jewish, Syro-Phoenician woman who asks Jesus to heal her daughter (Mark 7:24-30). He refuses, she pleads, and finally he agrees and heals her daughter—and at that moment, Christian commentaries inform us, Jesus was transformed from Jew to Christian. He abandoned his Jewishness and became a Christian by his finally agreeing to heal a non-Jew and thus overcoming the "fetters of Jewish nationalism," according to interpreters from the Church Fathers to the present day.

Christianity thus comes into being as a repudiation of Jewish nationalism, in the Christian imagination; Judaism is said to be particular, Christianity is said to be universal. As a result, Jewish statehood is not only a political issue, but is a deeply theological problem for Christians. If Christians reject Jewish nationalism on theological grounds, affirming Zionism becomes a repudiation of Jesus himself, regardless of any political or military decisions taken by Israel. As Jews, we can repudiate our claims to chosenness, uniqueness, special destiny, *Heilsgeschichte*, all we want, but Christian theology has created a mythic apparatus that will be difficult to dismantle, even if it undergoes a major theological reconfiguration.

Let me express a couple of concerns about issues that have arisen at this conference. First, I worry about Norman Podhoretz's calls for the elimination of Iran's nuclear capacity, not because I don't want that to happen, but because I think such calls give us a false sense of security. Destroying Iran's nuclear reactor will not eliminate the threat of terrorists with nuclear devices, nor will it address the aftermath of terrorism that such a military strike against Iran might provoke. The point of the twenty-first century is that military might cannot always defend against terror attacks nor prevail over guerilla warfare; deterrence does not have the power it had during the Cold War.

Second, Michael Walzer's call for a secular Jewish state like Norway is neither desirable nor realistic. We have long known that it is impossible to distinguish the secular from the religious when defining Jewishness. Will Passover once again become a festive celebration of political liberation movements? Such attempts, by some radical kibbutzim, for example, were utter failures and survive in memory as quaint, brief moments in Jewish history. Jewish identity is too deeply fused with religiosity, and particularly at this moment, with increasing numbers of Jews turning to religion, Walzer's call is anachronistic.

More important is the reality that most Jews who are deeply committed to Israel want a state and society infused with religion. The real problem is negotiating the extent of rabbinic authority, who qualifies for the rabbinate, and whether religious commitments can and should be imposed on the unwilling. Nearly all Jews want to experience Shabbat in Jerusalem, and feel uplifted by that experience, and many of us would like to have a mashgiach (rabbinic supervisor) not only in the restaurants and butcher shops, but also in the banks and businesses. Indeed, the rabbinate itself desperately needs rabbinic supervision to root out its corruption, manipulative displays of power, and insidious misogyny. The real problem is whether we can continue with a State of Israel whose Judaism is controlled by Orthodox—and, increasingly, Haredi—versions of Judaism, which are themselves Diasporic creations. It is absurd to attempt to create a secular Israel; what we need are ways to negotiate the nature and extent of the Jewish religiosity most of us dearly want.

Part of the blame for our present condition lies with our tendency in recent years, for understandable reasons, to speak of Israel primarily in political and military terms. As a result, we have neglected the deeper meaning of Israel to Jews, historically and spiritually, individually as well as communally, and for that we are paying a price. We have to return to the sense of purpose that is bound up with Israel, both as a state and as a beacon of moral and spiritual hope.

For most Jews, Israel is our source of inspiration. We know in the depths of our being that Israel is deeply entwined with Jewish history and faith, and is "endowed with the power to inspire" moments in which God's presence is palpable to us, as my father, Abraham Joshua Heschel, wrote. Israel, he said, "is a witness, an echo of eternity," which is why we "make aliyah," lifting ourselves to a higher plane, and why we send our young people there for an experience of inspiration that will affect them for a lifetime. We cannot negate the religious dimension of our lives and of our community, nor deny that being Jewish, for most of us, has always had a religious as well as an ethnic dimension. Let us not be naïve; modernity cannot be equated with secularism and religion is not going away. The time has come to end the strife between religious Jews and their opponents.

As various Israeli commentators have long noted, Israelis too often feel bereft of a connection with their Jewish heritage. The Zionist repudiation of the Diaspora has left many Israelis feeling uncertain of their Jewish identity. At the same time, Israeli observers like Hillel Halkin warn that those of us in the American Diaspora are missing the great Jewish historical adventure—and he is right. But that does not mean that, as one recently put it, "the Jews of Israel have let down the Jews of America." I may live in the U.S., but I only come alive in Israel—intellectually, culturally, spiritually—and so I know I am, Jewishly, here in America, a homo sacer, living a bare life. Max Nordau urged a Zionism that would restore our masculinity and heal our physical degeneracy, yet today Israel instead seems to be the hope for restoring our souls. If, as some Israelis are now urging, we abandon our sense of being special, unique, extraordinary within the history of the world—with all the attendant political privileges and miseries that come with uniqueness—we still cannot forget that we need moments of inspiration and idealism. We are indeed different from other groups in the United States—after all, Italians, Puerto Ricans and Norwegians have not faced genocide. What is important, not only for our young people, is that our discussions of Israel cannot only revolve around matters of politics and military security, issues that tend not to join us together but render us asunder. We must not neglect our ideals and our need for transcendence and inspiration.

We all agree that Israel's security is essential; what divides us is how best to achieve that security. Our divisions have created a hostility within the Jewish community that belies the unity of peoplehood that is the fundamental premise of Zionism. Our first task is to regain the trust and respect for fellow Jews who differ politically. Israel is here to unite us, not divide or demonize our viewpoints. In our postmodern, globalized world, in which shifts in religious commitments may occur with remarkable fluidity, and in which everyone, even the most devoutly Christian, seems to have Jewish family members, or establishes their identity by reference to Jews ("We're not Jews" is the title of Hanif Kureishi's short story about Anglo-Pakistanis), rules about who is a Jew and entitled to immediate citizenship in Israel beg for more nuanced understandings of Jewish identity.

Security is the sine qua non for Israel but is nonetheless insufficient. The security of Jewish statehood is unquestionable after the Shoah, but just as essential is the answer Israel can offer our battered sense of Jewish identity. Israel is not a panacea, but a challenge to our meager attention to the moral and spiritual question of what it means to be a Jew. We long to be ordinary, but our history has been extraordinary. How do we move beyond the ways Jewish history has been viewed, in attitudes mirroring views of Shylock as comical, tragic, or filled with pathos, and yet not arrive at utter indifference to the fate of the Jewish people?

The state of Israel functions in the imagination of most of the world as the Shylock who must be defeated for the self-gratification of the Gentile world. Shylock is called a figure of vengeance when it is in fact Portia and the Venetian court that wreak vengeful destruction on Shylock, speaking in the name of Christian mercy. We read Shylock not as wicked, but as exposing the wickedness of a Christian culture that calls him "alien." The play is not a reason for Jewish self-hatred; on the contrary, Shakespeare is demanding attention to the hostility that bred Portia, not Shylock. Culturally, Jews have often served similarly, as figures of inversion, calling attention to anti-Semitic stereotypes of us as projective pathologies of Gentile mentalities. Israel continues in that tradition, exposing Christian antagonism to Jewish nationalism and to fears of Jewish power and potential revenge for centuries of anti-Semitism.

The Merchant of Venice remains popular and resonant. Pockets still remain of audiences who laugh at Shylock, though now their contempt is for Israel, the contemporary surrogate for Shylock. The academic boycott of Israeli universities that is being promoted by some British academics represents a wish to return to the Jews' pre-Emancipation existence in Europe, precisely what gave rise to Zionism in the first place. Given the deeply entrenched British contempt for Israel among its chattering classes, it may be no wonder that some productions of The Merchant of Venice in England still evoke audience laughter at Shylock.

In reading *The Merchant of Venice* we can see the ways that Shylock mirrors the projected "jew" of the Christian imagination. We in the Diaspora still remain bound by that Shylock narrative, though today we might read Shylock not so much as an anti-Christ as an anti-Jesus, as I have argued elsewhere. To become freed from the constraints of that narrative is to enter Israel, to construct at long last an existence as Jews and Judaism liberated from the fetters of the idiosyncratic Christian master narrative of supersessionism. That audiences in Israel no longer resonate to Shakespeare's powerful play is a sign of hope that Israelis are lifting themselves out of the constraints that have been imposed on Jews for two thousand years. That absence of resonance may well be the first step toward a redefined Jewish identity that is a central component of Zionist thought. The goal is not to define the Israeli as a rejection of the Jewish, but as a new kind of Jewishness that offers inspiration not only through liberation but also as affirmation. To find Shylock irrelevant —that is the promise of Zionism; that is the gift of Israel.

Notes

1. Maria Edgeworth, *Harrington* (Orchard Park, NY: Broadview Press, 2004).
    John Gross, *Shylock: Four Hundred Years in the Life of a Legend* (London: Chatto & Windus, 1992).
2. Avraham Oz, "Transformations of Authenticity: The Merchant of Venice in Israel," in *The Merchant of Venice: Contemporary Critical Essays* (New York: St. Martin's Press, 1998).
3. Jeffrey Goldberg, *Prisoners : A Muslim and a Jew across the Middle East Divide* (New York: Alfred A. Knopf, 2006).
4. Abraham Joshua Heschel, Israel: An Echo of Eternity (New York: Farrar, Straus and Giroux, 1969).
5. Susannah Heschel, "From Jesus to Shylock: Configurations of Christians, Jews, and Gender in the Merchant of Venice," *Harvard Theological Review* 99, no. 4 (2006).

About the Contributors

Alan Dershowitz is the Felix Frankfurter Professor of Law at Harvard University. Arguably one of the world's best-known lawyers, his clients have included Natan Sharansky, Claus Von Bulow, Michael Milken, and Mike Tyson. Half of his cases are pro bono. Dershowitz is the author of more than twenty books of fiction and non-fiction. Among those relating to the Jewish community are *The Case for Peace: How the Arab Israeli Conflict can be Resolved, The Case for Israel, Why Terrorism Works, The Vanishing American Jew*, and the number-one bestseller, *Chutzpah*.

Yechiel Eckstein received his MA and rabbinic ordination from Yeshiva University and holds an MA degree from Columbia University, where he also studied for his doctorate. Founder and President of the International Fellowship of Christians and Jews, Rabbi Eckstein has devoted the past thirty years to building bridges between evangelical Christians and Jews, strengthening support for Israel, and other shared concerns. His organization has raised more than $200 million from Christians in support of various Jewish programs. Author of five books, Rabbi Eckstein serves on many boards, including the Jewish Agency in Israel and the Joint Distribution Committee. In 2004, he was named Goodwill Ambassador to Israel.

Leonard Fein is the founder of Moment magazine and served as its editor and publisher for ten years. He has also been a professor at MIT and Brandeis Universities. In 1985, Dr. Fein founded Mazon: A Jewish Response to Hunger and in 1996 he established the National Jewish Coalition for Literacy. The author of four books and nearly 1,000 articles, essays, and monographs, he writes a weekly, syndicated column for the Forward and is the recipient of four honorary doctorates.

Blu Greenberg, founding president of the Jewish Orthodox Feminist Alliance, is the author of a number of books, including, *On Women and Judaism: A View From Tradition, How to Run a Traditional Jewish Household, Black Bread: Poems After the Holocaust, and King Solomon and the Queen of Sheba.* She has long been active in interfaith work and serves on numerous boards, namely the National Jewish Family Center, the Covenant Foundation, the Jewish Book Council, and the Federation Task Force on Jewish Women. In 2000, Ms. Greenberg helped found and chaired the women's coalition, One Voice: Jewish Women for Israel.

Lawrence Grossman is editor of the American Jewish Year Book and associate director of research at the American Jewish Committee. The recipient of rabbinic ordination from Yeshiva University and holder of a Ph.D. in history from City University Graduate Center he has published over a hundred essays and reviews on Jewish life. Among his recent publications are "The Organized Jewish Community and Evangelical America," "Jews: Middle Atlantic and Beyond," "Mainstream Orthodoxy and the American Public Square," and "Jewish Religious Denominations." Dr. Grossman has authored the annual article on "Jewish Communal Affairs" in the *American Jewish Year Book* since 1988.

Hillel Halkin, author, essayist, and translator, has rendered over sixty works of fiction, poetry, and drama from Hebrew and Yiddish into English, including classic works by Agnon, Sholem Aleichem, Y. L. Peretz, and others. He was nominated for a Pulitzer Prize while serving as Israel correspondent for the *Forward* between 1993 and 1996. He is a regular contributor to *Commentary*, the *Jerusalem Post*, the *New Republic*, and the *New York Sun.* Among his many books are, *Letters to an American Jewish Friend: A Zionist Polemic*, winner of the National Jewish Book Award; *Beyond the Sabbath River*, winner of the Lucy Dawidowicz History Prize; and *A Strange Death: A Story Originating in Espionage, Betrayal, and Vengeance in a Village in Old Palestine.*

David Harris has been the executive director of the American Jewish Committee since 1990. A world traveler to hundreds of Jewish communities worldwide, monitoring their condition, he has been a driving force in many historic achievements, including the repeal of the infamous "Zionism is racism" U.N. resolution, the successful campaign to end Japan's adherence to the Arab economic boycott of Israel, and the rescue of Soviet and Ethiopian Jews. Mr. Harris has testified frequently on Jewish matters before the U.S. Congress, the U.N. Commission on Human Rights, and the French Parliament. A prolific author and commentator, his insightful biweekly AJC broadcasts are heard by an estimated 35 million listeners nationwide on the CBS Radio Network.

Samuel Heilman holds the Harold Proshansky Chair in Jewish Studies at City University Graduate Center and is Distinguished Professor at Queens College. He is the author of ten books, among them *Synagogue Life: The People of the Book, A Walker in Jerusalem, Defenders of the Faith: Inside Ultra-Orthodox Jewry, Portrait of American Jewry: The Last Half of the Twentieth Century, The Gate Behind the Wall*, and the recently published, *Sliding to the Right: The Contest for the Future of American Orthodoxy*. Professor Heilman has published many articles and reviews and is the editor of *Contemporary Jewry: The Journal of the Association for the Social Scientific Study of Jewry*.

Jeff Helmreich holds degrees in international affairs and law from Columbia and Georgetown Universities. His studies on the Middle East have been published by the Jerusalem Center for Public Affairs, and his articles have also appeared in the *Los Angeles Times*, the *Forward,* the *Jerusalem Post, Psychoanalytic Review*, and dozens of American Jewish periodicals. A former associate editor of the *Long Island Jewish World*, Mr. Helmreich served as spokesman and speechwriter for the Mission of Israel to the U.N., in both the Netanyahu and Barak governments. Most recently, he co-produced and co-wrote *Blood and Tears*, an acclaimed documentary about the Middle East conflict, which has been acquired by ThinkFilm and was recently released to theaters nationwide. Currently, Mr. Helmreich works in international law and jurisprudence.

William B. Helmreich is director of the Queens College Center for Jewish Studies, professor of sociology at CUNY Graduate Center and at City College of New York, and director of City College's Conflict Resolution Center. He is the author of nine books, including *Against All Odds: Holocaust Survivors and Successful Lives they Made in America*, winner of the National Jewish Book Award; *The Things they Say Behind your Back: Stereotypes and the Myths Behind Them*, and *The World of the Yeshiva: An Intimate Portrait of Orthodox Jewry*, and the editor of three volumes as well as general editor of Transaction Publisher's Classics in Judaica Series. Professor Helmreich has also been a visiting professor at Yale and Hebrew Universities. He has written for the *New York Times,*

Newsday, and the *Los Angeles Times*, and has appeared on *Oprah, Larry King Live, Sallye Jesse, CNN News*, and *NBC TV News*.

Susannah Heschel holds the Eli Black Chair in Jewish Studies in the Department of Religion at Dartmouth College. She is the author of *Abraham Geiger and the Jewish Jesus,* winner of the National Jewish Book Award, and a forthcoming book, *The Aryan Jesus: Christians, Nazis and the Bible*, as well as a co-editor of *Insider/Outsider: American Jews and Multiculturalism*, and publisher of a volume of her father, Rabbi Abraham Joshua Heschel's writings, *Moral Grandeur and Spiritual Audacity: Essays of Abraham Joshua Heschel*. Professor Heschel has also served as a visiting professor at Princeton University, the University of Frankfurt, the University of Cape Town and has been a member of the Academic Advisory Board of the Research Center of the U.S. Holocaust Memorial Museum. She has been a commentator on the *Jim Lehrer News Hour* and a contributor to the *Nation, Dissent, Commentary, Newsweek*, and *Tikkun*.

Malcolm Hoenlein has been executive vice chairman of the Conference of Presidents of Major Jewish Organizations since 1986, the umbrella group that represents fifty-two major Jewish groups. He completed his doctoral course work at the University of Pennsylvania's Department of International Relations and has taught in its Political Science Department. Mr. Hoenlein meets frequently with world leaders, government officials, and Jewish communities and serves on the boards of many leading organizations, including the Council on Foreign Relations. In 2002, he received a Doctorate of Humane Letters Honoria Causa from Yeshiva University.

Irving Louis Horowitz, the author of dozens of books and hundreds of articles, is the Hannah Arendt Distinguished Professor Emeritus of Sociology and Political Science at Rutgers University, where he also serves as Chairman of the Board of Transaction Publishers. He has published widely on Jewish affairs in publications ranging from *Congress Monthly* and *Midstream to Modern Judaism and Judaism*. His larger works— *Israeli Ecstasies/Jewish Agonies* and *Taking Lives: Genocide and State Power*, fifth edition, represent the range of his writings on the subject from 1958 to the present.

Norman Podhoretz, a holder of the Presidential Medal of Freedom, the nation's highest civilian honor, was editor in chief of *Commentary* from 1960-1995 and is now its editor at large, as well as an adjunct fellow at the Hudson Institute. He is the author of hundreds of articles and eleven books. His most recent volume, *World War IV: The Long Struggle Against Islamofascism*, was released in September 2007.

David Pryce-Jones read modern history at Oxford University. He is the author of thirteen books of non-fiction, among them, *The Closed Circle: An Interpretation of the Arabs, The Strange Death of the Soviet Union*, and *Paris in the Third Reich*. He has also published ten novels, most recently, *Safe Houses*. He contributes regularly to newspapers and magazines and is a senior editor of National Review.

Mark Rosenblum is director of the Jewish Studies Program, director of the Michael Harrington Center and associate professor of history, all of them at Queens College. He has written many scholarly and popular articles on the Middle East and has appeared as an analyst on the subject for CNN, CBS, NBC, MSNBC, and National Public Radio. Through the years, Professor Rosenblum has met with and advised most of the major players in the Middle East, including Ariel Sharon, Condoleeza Rice, Mahmoud Abbas, and King Abdullah II. He recently won a major Ford Foundation Grant for a Middle East reconciliation project as well as an award from the Clinton Global Initiative. In 1999, the *Forward* named him as one of the "fifty most influential American Jews" and in 2003 he received the Queens College President's Award for Excellence in Teaching.

David Saperstein has been director of the Religious Action Center of Reform Judaism for the past thirty years. Also an attorney, Rabbi Saperstein teaches seminars in both First Amendment State-Church Law and in Jewish Law at Georgetown University Law School. He represents the Union for Reform Judaism to Congress and the administration. Among the national boards on which he serves are, the NAACP, People for the American Way, the Leadership Conference on Civil Rights, and the Coalition on the Environment and Jewish Life. In 1999, Rabbi Saperstein was elected as the first chair of the U.N. Commission on International Religious Freedom.

David Schimel, the conference convener, is the holder of a J.D. from New York Law School, an MBA from Columbia University's Graduate School of Business, and an MIA from Columbia University's School of International Affairs. He is the co-author of *Trade for Freedom: Détente, Trade and Soviet Jews* and Editor of the *Jewish Political Chronicle*. Mr. Schimel is president of National Health Resources Inc. and a fellow of the New York Academy of Medicine. He is also a former Nassau County Human Rights Commissioner, past Associate President of the Long Island Regional Board of the Anti-Defamation League, and co-founder of the Committee for the Relocation of the U.S. Embassy to Jerusalem.

Michael Walzer has been a member of the faculty at Princeton University's Institute for Advanced Study since 1980. He is the author of many books, including, *Arguing About War, Just and Unjust Wars*, and *On Toleration*. He is also an editor of *Dissent*. Currently, Professor Walzer is working on two projects. One is an analysis of the toleration and accommodation of "difference" in all its forms. A second is a four-volume collaborative project focused on the history of Jewish political thought.

Jack Wertheimer is provost and professor of American Jewish history at the Jewish Theological Seminary of America. He is the author and editor of a dozen volumes, including, most recently, *Family Matters: Jewish Education in an Age of Choice*, and the forthcoming, *Imagining the American Jewish Community*. His recent research and publications have examined trends in Jewish philanthropy and synagogue life, communal approaches to Jewish education, and the national organizational structure of the American Jewish community.

Index